100

THINGS EVERY MAN
SHOULD KNOW

100

THINGS EVERY MAN SHOULD KNOW

Gareth May

◪ SQUARE PEG

Published by Square Peg 2013

2 4 6 8 10 9 7 5 3 1

First published in Great Britain in 2009 by Square Peg

Designed by www.unreal-uk.com

◙ SQUARE PEG

Random House, 20 Vauxhall Bridge Road,
London SW1V 2SA
www.rbooks.co.uk

Addresses for companies within The Random House Group Limited can be found at:
www.randomhouse.co.uk/offices.htm

The Random House Group Limited Reg. No. 954009

A CIP catalogue record for this book is available from the British Library

ISBN 9780224098885

The Random House Group Limited makes every effort to ensure that the papers used in its books are made from trees that have been legally sourced from well-managed and credibly certified forests. Our paper procurement policy can be found at:
www.randomhouse.co.uk/paper.htm

Printed and bound by CPI Group (UK) Ltd, Croydon, CR0 4YY

Dedication

For my Dad – the man I've always strived to emulate …

Contents

1.	How to iron a shirt like your mum	10
2.	How to hold chopsticks	11
3.	How to shine shoes like a squaddie	14
4.	The perfect shave	16
5.	How to slow dance with confidence	19
6.	How to choose and smoke a cigar	22
7.	How to open a bottle of champagne without blinding an innocent bystander	28
8.	How to hit the bullseye in darts	29
9.	How to open a jammed jam jar like a Greek god	32
10.	How to get hold of a good tradesman	33
11.	How to show your mum how iTunes works without strangling her with a USB cord	34
12.	How to sell all of your old toys on eBay	36
13.	How to win an arm wrestle	38
14.	Know your beef	40
15.	How to score a strike in ten-pin bowling	42
16.	Blagger's guide to playing rugby league	46
17.	What to look for when you buy your first second-hand car	48
18.	Essential painting and decorating tips	50
19.	Saving money on car maintenance	55
20.	How to organise a stag do like the best best man in history	56
21.	Blagger's guide to horse racing	58
22.	How to place a bet at the bookies	64
23.	How to moonwalk like Michael Jackson	66
24.	How to get off the phone from a cold caller	67
25.	How to get served at a busy bar	68
26.	How to put up shelves like a superhero	70
27.	How to act when you're in a posh restaurant for the first time	72
28.	Blagger's guide to wine	76
29.	How to make a bed like a nurse	78
30.	How to beat BO	79
31.	How to survive sleeping rough for a night	81
32.	How to impress your girlfriend's parents	82
33.	How to get a spider out of the bath without having a panic attack	84
34.	Spa etiquette	86

35.	Quick guide to shaving brushes	88
36.	Blagger's guide to golf scores	89
37.	Blagger's quick imperial to metric conversion guide	90
38.	How to change a tyre like an AA man	91
39.	How to tie the perfect full Windsor knot	94
40.	How to wolf whistle	96
41.	How to carve a chicken like your dad	98
42.	Sports injuries breakdown	99
43.	How to overtake like Lewis Hamilton	101
44.	How to tell if your pint of real ale is dodgy	102
45.	How to give a massage like a trained masseur	104
46.	How to pull the perfect sickie	106
47.	How to clean your bathroom, toilet and shower in a quarter of an hour	107
48.	How to out-buff a film buff when you know nothing about film	109
49.	How to wash your clothes like your mum	110
50.	Guide to washing symbols	111
51.	Blagger's guide to cricket fielding positions	113
52.	What flowers to buy for different occasions	114
53.	How to look after a beard	115
54.	How to survive your first poker night	116
55.	Facial grooming for grown-ups	117
56.	How to save money as well as the environment	119
57.	How to live on £40 a week and still have a social life	120
58.	How to rewire a plug without burning your house down	122
59.	How to prepare your CV for a job application	123
60.	Where to put things in the fridge	127
61.	Blagger's guide to knots	130
62.	How to buy a suit without getting ripped off	134
63.	Love on a budget: cheap but romantic dates	136
64.	Late and great gift ideas for girlfriends	137
65.	Survival guide to living at home with the folks	138
66.	How to give yourself a number one cut	140
67.	The perfect fry-up	141
68.	How to test for testicular cancer	142
69.	How to stay alive when you go shopping with the lady in your life	143
70.	How to get rid of sweaty armpits before a big meeting	144
71.	Blagger's guide to internet chat room slang	146
72.	Toolbox essentials	150
73.	How to give the perfect best man's speech	152
74.	How to get rid of shaving cuts in a hurry	154
75.	How to beat that Monday morning hangover from hell	155

76.	Prairie Oyster recipe	157
77.	First date survival guide	159
78.	How to sell your car	162
79.	How to build a campfire like a Boy Scout	165
80.	Getting the most out of being the designated driver	167
81.	How to do keepie uppies	169
82.	Blagger's guide to Texas Hold'em	171
83.	Festival essentials	177
84.	How to negotiate a pay rise with the boss	179
85.	Blagger's guide to fishing	182
86.	How to gut a fish	186
87.	How to dry your jeans in 15 minutes	187
88.	Coping with premature hair loss	188
89.	How to survive your first Starbucks experience	190
90.	How to perform the perfect golf swing	192
91.	Blagger's guide to apprentice slang	195
92.	How to behave in a job interview	196
93.	Make your own cider	198
94.	How to complain in a restaurant (without looking like a complete prat)	201
95.	How to fry the perfect steak	202
96.	How to taste wine in a restaurant	204
97.	Striking the cue ball in pool: how to generate different types of spin	205
98.	How to start a fire without matches or a light	207
99.	How to sharpen a knife using a whetstone	211
100.	Understanding your payslip	213

How to iron a shirt like your mum

To ensure the best iron finish, hang the shirt up on a hanger with the top button done up as this replicates the shape of the shirt when you wear it.

Whether you are a fisherman's wife or a bachelor running late for the office, the art of ironing a shirt is one which, once mastered, never fades, unlike a cheap short-sleever bought in the sale. Here's how to do it the good old-fashioned way.

Switch the iron on and allow to warm. If it's a steam iron, fill the water reservoir. Most shirts are made of cotton and iron better when slightly damp and at a high heat. If it's a dark colour, iron inside out to save the brightness, and if it is white make sure the iron is clean so you don't mark the innocent pallor of your shirt. Here's how to iron out those creases like a pro.

* **Collar** – Lay it flat, lengthways across the ironing board, and iron in one single motion back and forth a few times. Fold it over at the collar, as you would when you're actually wearing it, and run the iron over it again. Lift up and check the line.

* **Back** – Place the shirt back, or yoke on the ironing board, folded over just below the part which covers your shoulders and upper back. More often than not there will be a seam, so fold in accordance and iron with the point of the iron pushed up to the seam slowly moving towards the centre.

* **Sleeves** – Line them up one at a time by folding at the seam and laying them lengthways. Run the point of the iron down their side and across with a smooth run. Use your other hand to pull the fabric tight and iron the cuffs inside and out.

* **Front** – Place one side of the open shirt over the edge of the ironing board, with the end of the board sticking in the armhole and buttonholes facing widthways. Iron along the shoulder seam and around the collar. Then place the same side of the shirt, buttonholes lengthways, along the board. Lift and pull and iron until you come to the other side of the shirt. Iron in-between the buttons with the iron point and you're done.

How to hold chopsticks

'Man who catch fly with chopstick accomplish anything.'
Mr Miyagi

Customs are strange and wonderful things. In Britain using the last dregs of gravy or pinching the last Yorkshire pudding when you've already had the obligatory two might mean your host doesn't offer you any pork crackling the next time you pop round for a roast. Get your wires, or more specifically chopsticks, crossed in China, however, and you could be giving everyone around the table the sign of death.

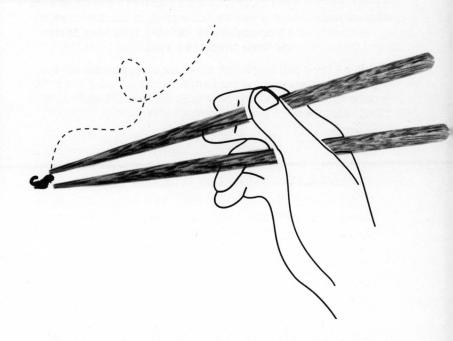

The people of Japan, China, Korea, Vietnam and Taiwan eat using chopsticks; that's a lot of disappointed people if you always ask for a fork. Joining their ranks is simple-ish.

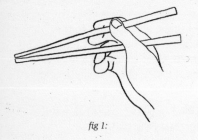

fig 1:

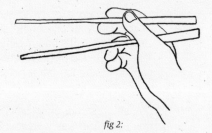

fig 2:

Pick up one chopstick like a pencil with the broad end resting into the V of skin where your thumb meets your index finger. Drop the narrow end down a finger so that it rests against the side of your end knuckle. It should fit there snugly and firmly. Pick up the second chopstick with your index finger and middle finger using your thumb to hold it in place. Adjust until their ends are touching and even. Do this swiftly and smoothly if you want to look like a real pro. When you start to eat, the bottom chopstick should always stay still and the top chopstick should pivot. This is done by slowly moving the knuckle joint at the end of your middle finger; straighten to widen and bend inwards to clamp together. Only move your thumb when you need to realign the chopsticks.

As a beginner, you might find it easier to hold the chopsticks nearer to the middle or closer to the tips. As you grow in confidence however, you should hold them further towards the blunt end as it's considered polite to keep your hands as far away from the food as possible.

A few more things to consider:

* Picking up food should be done gently; don't apply too much pressure or be tempted to stab at your chow mein in desperation.

* When taking from communal bowls use the broad ends of the chopsticks so you don't pass on the germs from your mouth.

* When eating rice either use a shovelling motion or pack it together into a small mouthful. Don't be afraid to lift the bowl up to your chin.

* Noisily slurping up your noodles is perfectly OK.

A few cultural chopstick no-nos:

*   Don't lick, stab, rake or point your chopsticks at fellow diners. This is a no-no-no.

*   Never stick your chopsticks straight down into the rice so they stand upright. It's bad manners because it will remind Chinese or Japanese diners of the incense burned when mourning a relative – not something too many people like thinking about while they're eating their tea.

*   Do not cross your chopsticks. In China this is a symbol of death and won't go down well with your foreign business partners.

*   It is usual to hold your chopsticks in your right hand. For some holding them in the left hand symbolizes dispute and could land you in A & E with a chopstick in the eye.

*   Do not pass food round the table with your chopsticks. In Japanese mourning rituals bones are passed between family members with chopsticks.

*   Resist tapping the edge of your bowl with your chopsticks. This is considered rude because it is what beggars do and might also lead you to break out in a verse of 'Why are we waiting? Because we're salivating. Oh, why are we waiting...'

*   Try not to drop your chopsticks. This is considered bad luck and a little bit manky if you pick them up off the floor and continue using them to eat.

Remember – using chopsticks is like riding a bike. Once you get the hang of it, you never forget. Keep some chopsticks from your next take-away delivery and practise, practise and practise again in the comfort and privacy of your own home until your chopstick prowess would make Mr Miyagi proud. And what's more, you'll never have to buy a can of fly spray again.

How to shine shoes like a squaddie

They say you can tell a lot about a man from the state of his shoes. So pay heed. Spitting on a piece of loo roll and dabbing at the leather like your nan trying to rid your cheek of tomato ketchup won't cut it.

You will need:

* Newspaper
* Polish brush
* Black wax polish for black leather, brown for brown
* Horsehair shine brush
* Water sprayer
* Cotton balls – a piece of cloth wrapped around two fingers or a sock pulled over your hand will do.
* Shoe cloth (or use an old T-shirt or some nylon tights)
* Old toothbrush

Step 1.
Spread some newspaper out across the floor or table.

Step 2.
Remove the shoelaces. Use a brush or damp cloth to remove all dirt and dust from the shoe's surface. If your shoes are slightly damp, let them dry before putting the polish on.

Step 3.
Use the polish brush to apply the wax in small circular movements. Work round the shoe until the polish is spread evenly all over the leather.

Step 4.
Work the wax into the seams with the old toothbrush.

Step 5.
Leave to dry at room temperature for 15 minutes.

14

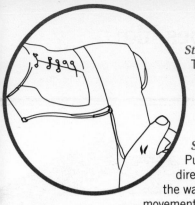

Step 6.
Take your horsehair brush and shine away like a madman until you've covered the whole shoe. This will remove all excess wax. Spritz the shoe with water from a sprayer once in a while to produce a better shine.

Step 7.
Put about a pea-sized amount of wax or polish directly on to a damp cotton wool ball. Massage the wax into the leather with small circular movements, paying special attention to the heel and toe. Repeat, using a fresh cotton ball each time, until you've got the right amount of shine on your shoe. Don't stop until you can watch TV in the reflection of the polish on your shoes. This could take up to 15 shines so be patient.

Step 8.
Use a clean cloth, a sock, an old T-shirt or your girlfriend's nylon tights – when she's not wearing them of course – and buff up the shoe vigorously. Thread the shoelaces back through their holes, put the newspaper in the bin and twinkle toes is ready for anything.

Choosing your polish:

For black shoes, use black polish. The correct shade of brown, for brown shoes. Keep separate polish brushes for brown and black shoes.

Cream and paste polish – for fine leather. Keeps it flexible and moisturized, allowing it to breathe. Exaggerates colour and extends shoe life.

Wax polish – easily covers scuffs and shines the best. Can dry out the leather.

Liquid polish – fast shine but can crack and dry out the leather.

Bee's wax – melt in a tablespoon and apply as above. Similar effects to wax polish.

If the wax polish is hard and tough strike a match and pass it over the wax until it catches alight. Once all the wax is burning place the lid over the tin and snuff out the flames. Remove the lid carefully and once the minuscule mushroom cloud dissipates you'll be left with a smooth wax ready for application.

Quick tip for shiny shoes in seconds:

If you're late for a posh do, peel a banana and dash the inside of the skin over the leather. Remove flecks of banana, tie your shoelaces and shoot out the door ... not forgetting to eat the banana on the way.

The perfect shave

Chad Gillette was a funny old sausage. Despite being heralded as a 'king' – of the shaving world at least – Gillette died a discontented and frustrated man.

A staunch socialist, in 1894 he wrote a book entitled *The Human Drift* which suggested competition was the root of all evil; this from the man who bought out smaller companies so that his would survive. He was a razor-sharp competitor who did not want to compete and in the end, with the Wall Street crash of 1929 and the knowledge that he had become a figurehead of capitalism, it was he who lost. Here's a guide to the perfect wet shave.

How to shave:

1. Wash your face with a mild soap. This will remove any dirt and oil which may get trapped in your pores or reduce the impact of your razor. Pat your face dry but ensure it is still moist.

2. Preferably shave after a hot shower or smother your face with a warm flannel. The warm water and steam will form a thin film between skin and lather, which allows the blade to 'skim' over your skin rather than pull at the hairs. Warm water also softens your bristles, relaxes your facial muscles and opens your pores; all in all the perfect formula for a smoother, closer shave.

3. A little pre-shave oil can be used – this can help prevent cuts and irritation as it helps soften the stubble, giving a smoother shave.

4. Shave over a sink filled with warm water and steam your face while you shave. Lather up – soak your shaving brush in the sink of hot water, then take it out and allow all excess water to pour out.

5. Squirt a small amount of shaving gel – a thimble's worth is about right – into the palm of your hand, or use a tub of shaving cream. Swirl the brush in circular motions in the foam in your hand, or directly in the tub, until a creamy lather is formed on the bristles.

6. Splash warm water on your face. Apply the foam with the brush using circular motions over your skin, against the direction of hair growth. Finish with an upward stroke – this will lift the hairs away from your skin, ready for trimming. This should take up to three minutes; a thorough lather leads to a thorough shave. Your face should now be covered in a thin but opaque layer of white foam.

7. Always use a sharp and clean razor. Blunt razors miss hairs and require you to go back over the same spot again, causing razor burn. Warm the razor in the sink or run it under the hot tap prior to shaving.

8. Shave in short strokes going with the grain, or, in other words, in the same direction as the hair growth. If you shave against the grain, the hairs are pulled sharply away from your face, causing cuts, razor burn and ingrown hairs. Glide the razor lightly over the skin. You can hold your skin taut with your free hand, especially when it comes to doing your cheeks.

9. Do your sideburns first, followed by your jawline, then the neck. The area around your lips and chin should be left till last – these are the toughest hairs on your face so need longer to become softened by the shaving foam.

10. Be guided by the contours of your face. Look at your face carefully in the mirror and see which way your hairs grow. Contours and grains change all over your face. No face is the same.

11. Rinse the razor in hot water after every stroke; hairs caught in the blades cause you to miss spots and you'll have to go over the same area several times.

12. If necessary, add a splash of warm water to your face and lather the area again with your brush.

13. When you have finished, splash cold water on your face to close your pores, reduce irritation and to remove any traces of shaving foam from around your ears and under your chin.

14. Pat your face dry with a soft clean towel. Don't scrub or rub your face or you'll end up looking like a beetroot.

15. Rinse, dry and put away your razor and brush

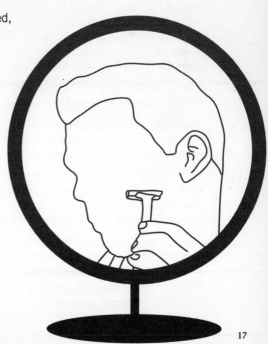

Advanced tips:

* **Don't use a cheap or disposable razor; treat yourself to a decent one. Under no circumstances should you use your mum's or girlfriend's.**

* Glycerine-based shaving creams cause less skin irritation than cooling gels as they don't close the pores mid-shave.

* If you shave every day, apply a moisturizer post-shave. Shaving removes the outermost layer of skin cells so give your skin a break once in a while and let the beard grow.

* Exfoliating your skin pre-shave will give you a closer shave.

* Some testify to re-lathering up and softly running the razor against the grain for the closest shave.

* Multi-blades offer control but don't follow the contours of your face as well as a single-bladed razor which requires more skill but will reward you with a closer shave.

* If you've run out of shaving cream, in an emergency you can use olive oil instead. Never use hand soap or Vaseline.

* Ingrown hairs should be pulled out with a pair of tweezers and then shaved over as normal and they should disappear within six weeks.

Aftershave tips:

* Despite Macaulay Culkin looking cool slapping aftershave on in *Home Alone*, you shouldn't actually scream in agony when you apply aftershave. If it stings, don't use it.

* Oily skin should be treated with aftershave that's made to keep skin dry. Dry skin should be treated with one that moisturizes.

* Alcohol-based aftershaves will tighten your skin and dry it out, leaving you looking like Joan Rivers.

How to slow dance with confidence

As the lights dim and the music slows, unless your name is Patrick Swayze, the girl of your dreams won't be expecting you to grab her hand, say 'Nobody puts Baby in a corner' and run onto the dance floor like the winners of Strictly Come Dancing. *However, once you've politely asked the question and she's said 'yes', taking a girl confidently by the hand and leading her up to dance with open shoulders and a powerful stride will fill her with awe and – hopefully – admiration.*

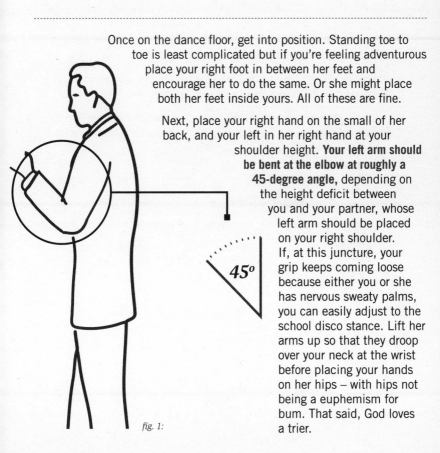

Once on the dance floor, get into position. Standing toe to toe is least complicated but if you're feeling adventurous place your right foot in between her feet and encourage her to do the same. Or she might place both her feet inside yours. All of these are fine.

Next, place your right hand on the small of her back, and your left in her right hand at your shoulder height. **Your left arm should be bent at the elbow at roughly a 45-degree angle,** depending on the height deficit between you and your partner, whose left arm should be placed on your right shoulder. If, at this juncture, your grip keeps coming loose because either you or she has nervous sweaty palms, you can easily adjust to the school disco stance. Lift her arms up so that they droop over your neck at the wrist before placing your hands on her hips – with hips not being a euphemism for bum. That said, God loves a trier.

fig. 1:

45°

A waltz is the simplest of all the classic dance steps, and the rumba and Argentine tango are very erotic, but if you can't dance ballroom, now isn't the time to start experimenting with complicated moves picked up from Len Goodman. Simply move rhythmically in time to the music – one step per beat – leading your lady by gently pulling and pushing her right hand and taking small steps. Or, if the dance floor is polished, sliding your feet forwards and backwards, and from side to side, moving in a small square.

Patience is the key. Don't start to jolt and jerk her about like you're trying to move a wardrobe round the room; allow your weight to lead her and remember to smile. Whisper to her how beautiful she looks or stare into her eyes (but not too hard or too long, lest she starts to worry she's in the grip

 YES

of a potential stalker). Holding out for two or three songs in this romantic stance will make her heart skip a few beats.

Know when to leave the dance floor and retire to a table: don't show foolish tenacity if the music changes tempo and 'Come on Eileen' blasts out of the stereo. And definitely make a run for it before the conga starts up and you get lumbered with Old Granny Hubbard's rear end.

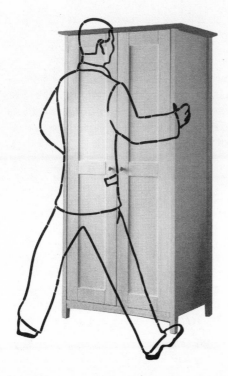

How to choose and smoke a cigar

Graduation. A new job. The signing of Cristiano Ronaldo on ISS Superstar Soccer. A cigar is the emblem of celebration. Prepared properly they should take anything from thirty minutes to an hour to smoke, so here's how. Sit back and enjoy without dissolving into a spluttering paroxysm of coughing.

Choosing your cigar:

* Cigars, like fine wines and brandies, come in different strengths: mild, medium-bodied and strong.

* Ask a reputable tobacconist for recommendations, or you might like to buy a six-cigar sampler box from a good brand to start off with.

* A simple rule when choosing a cigar is the colour of the outer tobacco leaf, or wrapper. The darker the cigar wrapper, the stronger the taste. For the seasoned cigar connoisseur, stronger cigars have more depth and nuances of flavour. For the beginner, however, stick to the lighter and milder cigars.

* Longer, thinner cigars have a less intense flavour and strength, so are better for beginners.

* Some suggested brands for beginners are Baccarat Luchadores and Flor de Oliva torpedo.

* The price of cigars varies hugely depending on the brand, size and country of origin. In general, Cuban cigars are considered best quality, and a Montecristo is la crème de la crème. Expect to pay anything between £10 and £40 for a single top-range cigar. The Gurkha 'Her Majesty's Reserve' cigar comes in at a whopping $750 per smoke.

KNOW YOUR CIGAR

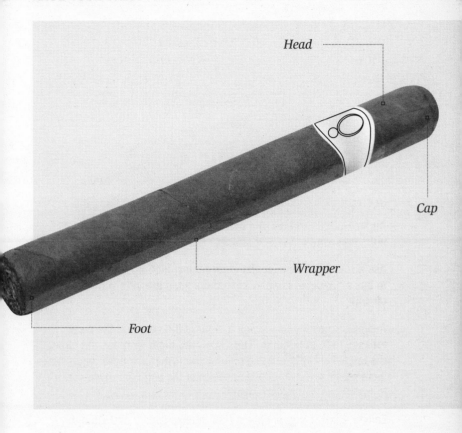

Head – the end located nearest the sticker with the logo on it. The bit you put in your mouth, basically.

Foot – you guessed it. The other end. The one you light.

Cap – a roll of tobacco, which is stuck to the head of the cigar to keep the wrapper in place. Only present on hand-rolled cigars.

Wrapper – the outer leaf of tobacco wrapped tightly round the binding and inner leaves of the cigar, or the 'filler' – the wrapper should be smooth, even-toned and silky smooth to the touch. Look out for any tears, discoloration or drying on the wrapper.

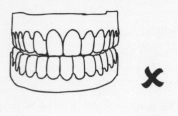

✗

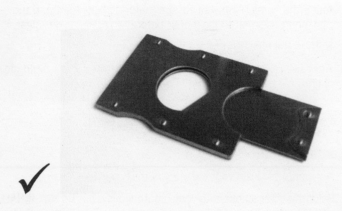

✓

How to cut a cigar:

You might have seen it in the movies, but never bite the end off a hand-rolled cigar. Use a cigar cutter.

1. Grip the cutter with your strongest hand between thumb and forefinger.

2. Hold the cigar in your free hand with the head facing the cutter.

3. Find the line where the cap ends; you need to cut before this line, leaving about half a centimetre of the cap intact.

4. Insert the cigar. You can close one eye to assist in your lining up the cigar properly.

5. Steady the cigar.

6. Cut down all the way through the cigar with a strong, quick, precise cut. Don't pussy-foot about when cutting as any fumbling or indecision may cause the cigar to unfurl.

How to light a cigar:

1. Use a wooden match or butane lighter.

2. Place the cigar in your mouth holding it between your thumb and index finger a couple of centimetres from the head. If your cigar is as big as a baguette, use as many fingers as it takes.

3. Light the lighter or strike the match and place the cigar tip so it is hovering a few millimetres above the flame – don't let it actually touch the flame. Also wait for the match to fully light and the phosphorous smell to disappear before taking it to your cigar.

4. Puff on the cigar and rotate it at the same time.

5. After twenty seconds or so the outer rim of the cigar should glow slightly. At this point you will be able to draw smoke.

How to smoke a cigar:

1. As you puff, rotate your cigar every thirty seconds or so.

2. Take the cigar smoke into your mouth slowly, but **DO NOT INHALE**, or you'll choke like you did when you took your first toke on that cigarette behind John's dad's garage. The whole point of cigar-smoking is to savour the taste in your mouth and **NOT** to inhale. The nicotine is absorbed through the mouth and nose's membranes and is so strong that you will get a buzz even though you are not inhaling the smoke into your lungs. See **HEALTH WARNING** below!

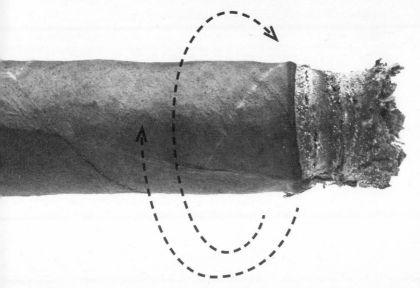

3. Savour the taste of the cigar in your mouth and then blow the smoke out.

4. Don't smoke too fast – you'll burn the tobacco and ruin the flavour – or too slow – you'll have to keep relighting it. About a puff per minute is perfect.

5. When the ash finger exceeds a centimetre it should fall off of its own accord. However, the longer the ash finger, the higher quality the cigar. Don't tap your cigar on the edge of the ashtray as you do when smoking a cigarette, but if the ash doesn't fall off by itself, lightly shake the cigar until it does.

6. Once you're down to the last five centimetres you'll begin to get an aftertaste and the cigar will get hotter. That's the end of the road for this cigar.

Don't stub out a burning cigar. Simply place it in an ashtray and it will automatically stop burning. Once cold, empty the ashtray and dispose of the cigar stubs to minimize odours. Stubbing out a lit cigar will stink the whole place out with an acrid smell which will linger for several weeks.

Advanced tips for the novice cigar connoisseur:

* Smoke a varied selection of mild single cigars at first; you don't want to blow a whole month's wages on a box of Cubans if they make you throw up.

* Always inspect the wrapper – not the packet, the outer layer of the cigar – for rips and tears. Roll the cigar between finger and thumb; if there are any hard areas the cigar might be 'plugged' and unsmokable, any soft spots and it might not be packed tight enough and won't give a good draw.

* To prevent drying, only remove a cigar from its packet when you mean to smoke it.

* Have a glass of cold water to hand to sip between puffs. This will help cleanse your palate and might also help if the whole experience makes you feel sick.

* Brandy, Scotch and coffee compliment a cigar. If you're trying out several cigars don't vary your drink as this can affect the flavour of the cigar.

HEALTH WARNING

It is not unusual for novice cigar-smokers to feel sick or actually be sick as a result of their first taste of a cigar. This is due to nicotine overdose. An average cigarette contains 1mg of nicotine. A large cigar such as a Torpedo or a Churchill, on the other hand, may contain as much as 400mg of nicotine, or the equivalent of smoking twenty cigarettes at once.

How to open a bottle of champagne without blinding an innocent bystander

When popping open an ice-cold bottle of bubbly, never aim it at the waiter, your granny or the very expensive chandelier hanging in the dining room. A male nemesis, an unruly houseguest or a strategically placed apple on Debbie McGee's head, however, are perfectly legitimate targets.

Here's how to open a bottle of Bolly like you've been drinking the stuff your whole life:

1. Remove the foil, revealing the wire cage covering the cork below. Loosen and remove the wire cage by twisting the ends until they become free.

2. Place a dish towel or fabric napkin over the bottleneck, fully covering the cork.

3. Angle the bottle towards a wall and firmly but slowly twist the cork out with your thumb controlling the pop – the cloth will help give leverage. Don't remove your thumb at any point – until you hear the pop. Don't pull the cork out once you feel it getting loose; just twist the bottle or the cork itself until it comes free.

4. When pouring champagne, angle the neck of the glass slightly to avoid getting a glass full of bubbles.

5. If the glass does fizz up with bubbles, simply place a clean finger in the middle of the champagne and the bubbles will miraculously disappear.

How to hit the bullseye in darts

They might not have the rugged good looks and muscle tone of a Wimbledon champion or Brazil international. They might not be picked to model topless for the new fragrance of RightGuard. And they might huff and puff their way up to the oche and groan when they bend over to pick up a bounced-out dart, but for all that, darts players stand alone in the pantheon of sport's history, for darts is the only sport in which the training regime positively demands necking limitless amounts of beer.

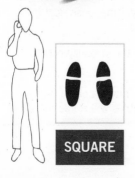

Grab your pint and step up to the oche like a world champion.

Stance. Take a manly swig of your ale, then take position, standing side on to the dart board, with your leading foot on the oche. Your other foot should be behind you, about shoulder width apart. Distribute your weight evenly; don't lean forward as this will unbalance you. Stand up straight, shoulders back and in line with the board. A steady arm is the key to accurate throwing. Keep both feet planted to the ground and try not to lift your heels as you throw. Instead, focus on holding your body fixed and steady.

SQUARE

SIDEWAYS

ANGLED

Grip. Balance the dart evenly in your hand and find where the centre of gravity is. Roll the dart towards your fingertips with your thumb and place the pad of your thumb just behind the located centre of gravity. Use only two fingers and your thumb to lightly grip the dart, your 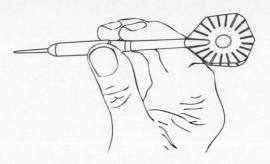 index and middle finger with your middle finger at the front. Bend all your fingers with the tips facing the board. Your grip should be firm but relaxed, so if your fingers start going white, you're holding the dart too hard. Fold any fingers that aren't gripping the dart away from the dart. Don't touch the flight, or you'll put spin on the dart and it will shoot off into somebody's pint. This will earn you a black eye, not a bullseye.

Set-up. Line up the dart with the bullseye. Hold the dart with your elbow straight, the dart held level and never at an angle. Keep it pointed straight at the board and never downwards, no matter what part of the board you are aiming for. Keep your eye, the dart and the target in one long line. Keep your elbow pointing at the floor. Your shoulders should be at an angle of 50–80 degrees to the board.

Pullback. The power for your throw comes from your wrist, fingers and arm. Pull your hand back towards your shoulder and aim the dart just above the bullseye. Arch your wrist slightly to elevate the dart. Bend your knees. Focus on your target and slowly move your arm into position. Pull back as far as is possible without slipping a disc.

Release. Thrust your arm forward and release the dart. Except for your throwing arm your body should make no other movement. Your elbow will flex slightly at the highest point and towards the end of the throw – that's when you should release the dart, not before. Don't flick your wrist, just use your arm – the pros do this to increase acceleration but until you have the throw sorted it's best left to the experts. Always keep the dart parallel with the floor and release all your fingers at the same time.

Follow through. Your hand should point slightly below the bullseye and your arm should be straight. Hold this final stance – this doesn't help the accuracy but you'll look cool.

Advanced tips:

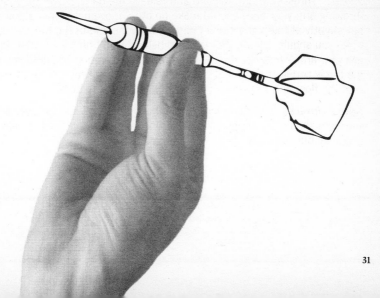

Practise your throw. Try to hit the same spot several times in a row. Once you've nailed a good stance, grip and throwing technique, with practice you will improve your accuracy.

Watch the pros and study their grips and stances. Copy them until you find one that works for you.

Check your stance by throwing with your eyes closed – you'll be able to tell if you're moving with the deftness of a Jedi.

Check how far your dart is entering the board. The barrel should not be touching the board – if it is going in too deep, you are throwing too hard.

Do some stretches before playing to relax and warm the muscles.

Sandpaper the ends of your darts to keep the tips sharp. Place onto the sandpaper and rotate like you're sharpening a pencil.

Breathe – practising your breathing technique as in yoga will help keep you centred, focused and calm.

How to open a jammed jam jar *like a Greek god*

Hercules fought off the hounds of hell. Atlas held the heavens on his shoulders. Zeus... well, Zeus just sat around looking hard. But when the Greek gods gathered at the bottom of Mount Olympus, munching crumpets and drinking tea, there was one feat of strength that outdid all three: the mighty feat of opening the jammed jam jar.

Here's how to succeed where gods have failed and enjoy your toast and jam:

1. Tap a spoon around the lid top or tap the lid against the table edge. This should release some air pressure and allow you to pop it open first try. If still resistant, use a teaspoon or flat-head screwdriver to lift the lid up slightly at several points around the lid to break the vacuum.

2. If you're still struggling, wrap a damp tea towel round the lid and have another go. If that still fails, wrap a thick rubber band round the lid edge to give you increased purchase.

3. Toast going cold? Still no jam? Run the lid under hot water for at least a minute. This should expand the metal so it will slide off with a twist.

If all else fails, stab a sharp knife through the lid. This will break the vacuum, disperse the pressure and allow you to have a jam sandwich at long last.

How to get hold of a good tradesman

Cowboy builders. They drink all your tea. Eat all your Bourbon Creams. Put you off whistling and early mornings for life. And leave you with a half-built kitchen and a pathological distrust of anyone with a pencil tucked behind one ear.

Save your biccies and find yourself an honest brickie:

* Get recommendations from friends and relatives or even next-door neighbours for a job that is similar to yours.

* Get other plumbers or builders to recommend someone. Shops may also make recommendations. If you've bought a new sink from the local hardware store they might be able to inform you of a trusty tradesman.

* Feel free to ask for a list of references. Work your way from the middle of the list and call at least three or four people.

* Follow up word-of-mouth references also. If your Auntie Marjorie says your Uncle Steve said Great-Grandma Hilda heard Father Lovecraft had his kitchen done by a nice bloke from Chepstow, ring the reference up and find out the facts.

* Get at least three quotes or estimates for the job.

* Get a written quote including a fixed deadline, an on-site assessment and VAT. Never go ahead on a verbal agreement only; they could still be there after the Rio Olympics.

* A good tradesman is normally busy. If they're free straight away, be wary.

* Work out a payment schedule. Be dubious if they want you to pay in cash and deliver the money in a black bin liner to a deserted garage out of town.

* Always being available via phone or email shows a commitment to new customers and an organized approach to work.

* Keep a file of work being done and receipts etc. This will aid you should you get into a dispute.

How to show your mum how iTunes works without strangling her with a USB cord

There's no doubt that mothers are the greatest thing since sliced bread. In fact, they probably sliced the bread in the first place. But that doesn't mean there aren't moments in our lives when we would sooner starve than give mother dearest a helping hand.

These situations normally involve technology and, more specifically, computers. Or worse still, the double whammy of computer and iPod. Brace yourself, take a deep breath and maybe a stiff drink – follow the step-by-step instructions below and before you know it you will have an eternally grateful mum loudly singing along to her Dido tracks and boasting about her downloads.

Download iTunes from www.apple.com/itunes/download. Choose your operating system, tick the box and enter her email address to begin the download. Once downloaded, an icon called iTunes Setup will appear on her desktop. Double click and start installation. Follow the on-screen instructions, shushing your mum every time she asks you a question even a leading scientist at NASA couldn't answer. Now set up a desktop shortcut, make iTunes the default music player and apply for Apple software updates. Be considerate; remember that when it comes to computers your mum has the mental capacity of an orang-utan. Actually that's probably a little unfair to the ape.

Once installed, iTunes will scan her hard drive for any music files and import them. Get your mum to fetch her favourite CDs and open iTunes. Making sure you're online, insert each CD and wait for the computer to connect to the internet. iTunes will then automatically collect information from the Compact Disc Database (CDDB for short) and display each CD's name, artist and song titles. This will make your mum say: 'Oh. How did it do that?' Just ignore her and click on the bottom right-hand corner button marked 'Import'. The CD will now be imported. You will know the process is complete when her computer chimes, to which your mum will respond by saying: 'Oh. What was that?' You will smile fondly and say nothing.

Connect her iPod via a USB port. Make sure she knows where to plug it in – and follow the instructions. iTunes will download all the songs in the library on to her iPod. Don't do anything else while it does this, just be patient and glare at your mum. She can now make some choices about what content she wants to sync by clicking the tabs at the top of the iPod window. Click 'Apply' at the bottom right-hand corner of the window once she has finished and her James Blunt, Neil Diamond and Katie Melua albums will be transferred to her iPod.

Create an iTunes Store account. Choose the iTunes Store option in the left-hand menu and click 'Sign In'. Choose 'Create New Account'. Agree to the iTunes Store's terms, on the next screen enter your mum's email and get her to give you a password. Suggest your mum chooses a member of the family's date of birth for her password as this is a good way to guarantee she'll never forget it. Either that or Nick Berry, *Robson and Jerome* or Ross Kemp should suffice. For the secret question, type in: 'Which amazing son helped you install iTunes?' and tick the newsletters option. Click 'Continue' and enter your mum's billing details including her address, her card number and security code. At this point you can also get her to make you a cup of tea, write down her card details and get your dad into a whole lot of trouble. 'But darling, I swear I've never even heard of barbarasbigbouncyones.com.'

How to sell all of your old toys on eBay

Grab your He-Man, Thundercat, Stretch Armstrong or Space Hopper, give them a good clean and a kiss and prepare them for their big sendoff. Avoid eye contact. They're never going to forgive you for this; all those years of joy sold for £5 plus postage and packaging.

Register with the site. Get online and click 'Register' to create a seller's account. Choose an online ID: this is the name other people will see you as so don't choose an embarrassing nickname from school. 'Pissy Pants' or 'Twinkle Nuts' won't inspire customer confidence. Once you've filled in the registration form you'll receive an email asking you to confirm your account. Confirm, return to the site, register your billing with PayPal and you're done. Now you're ready to start selling.

Research. Search for similar items on eBay and note down selling prices and info. This will help you with the title, description, price, payment method, postage cost and photo forms you'll need to fill in.

List your toy for sale. Use key words in your 'Listing Title', including the make and model of the toy, any other key details such as the colour and the recommended age range of the toy, dimensions, interesting features and any damage, repairs, etc. – you are limited to 55 words, so make them count. The more key detail you add, the better chance of a sale. See below for eBay jargon.

Take a photo of your toy. You will need a digital camera for this part. Use a plain white or dark wall as a backdrop (pin up a white sheet if necessary). Keep the photo clear and clean, and shoot the item head on with no other items in the picture other than the toy you are selling. Use this shot as your 'Gallery Photo'. Take a few more photos at different angles, zooming in on particular features or any damage or repairs. Make sure the lighting is right – shoot the toy outside in good light if possible, or if not, take the photo in a bright room in daylight and light the shot with a few desk lamps inside. Try to avoid shadows and switch off the flash on your camera.

Add a photo. Download the pictures onto your hard drive, choose the 'Bring your item to life' option on the 'Sell your item' section of the site and click 'Add pictures'. Browse to select the pictures on your hard drive, then select and click 'OK'.

Once listed. eBay will automatically categorize your item. The total cost of selling the item is the Insertion Fee; this is the charge eBay make for listing your item on their site and is matched to the starting price. Unless you're selling a priceless Steiff bear, keep the starting price for your cuddly friends reasonable. Chances are your Stretch Armstrong's emotional value won't always translate into hard cash.

The sale. When a listing is successful you'll get an email from eBay detailing your buyer's payment method and postage address. Once you receive the money, package the items carefully and take them to the post office.

Wave goodbye to childhood innocence. Get thinking about how to blow the proceeds in a suitably grown-up fashion.

SOME EBAY SELLER JARGON:

New in Box (NIB). Informs the buyer the original packaging has not been either tampered with or opened since purchase. Effectively, brand new and mint condition.

Gently used (GU). Taken out of the box but well looked after with no marks or damage. Pretty much original condition.

Excellent. Well kept, clean, but may have small scratches and marks.

Very good. Scratches but no major dents or discrepancies.

Good. Some scratches and dents.

Fair. Well used and therefore well worn, toys with dents and many scratches.

Poor. Highly damaged and possibly even broken but may be good for spare parts.

How to win an arm wrestle

Winner

Settling a dispute like a man can be a nasty pursuit. Sometimes it's best to turn tail and shout, 'Leg it' at the top of your voice. Other times, if you're feeling particularly upbeat about your chances of outdoing a fellow male, why not challenge him to an arm wrestle to settle the argument? Just don't bottle it at the last minute and ask for a thumb war instead.

Here are the key factors to ensure you bring this one home:

Feet. Sit as close to the table as possible, and if you're right-handed put your right foot firmly on the ground as far as is comfortable in front of your left, left in front of right if you're left-handed. Hook your other foot around the chair leg for added support as you wrestle.

Grip. 'Wrapping' your thumb is the most effective way to grip your opponent's hand. Reach for their hand, grip as normal but rather than having your thumb resting over both your and your opponent's hand tuck, or 'wrap', it under your fingers.

Arm placement. When you place your elbow on the table keep your upper arm close to your chest. This gives stability and limits shaking and also aligns your arm with your body to give you added power. Keep your arm straight in front of your shoulders. Never let your arm leave this position.

Use your shoulders and upper torso. Don't push with your arm alone, but use all the power from your upper body. Your arm merely channels that power. After all, your biceps are nothing in comparison to all the muscles in your shoulders and back. Unless you're Rafael Nadal who has abnormal biceps the size of a young child's head.

Arm-wrestling moves:

Back pressure. Pull your opponent's arm across the table towards you. With his body stretched, and with the side pressure you're placing on his arm, he'll lose the power of his body and have to fight you with his arm alone. Be quick, otherwise he'll use the same move on you first.

Hook 1   *Hook 2*   *Top roll*

The Hook. Curl your wrist around your opponent's hand – the most common form of arm-wrestling move – and manoeuvre your body over your arm. Keep wrist contact steady as you wrestle so that the power is delivered through the wrist rather than your arm.

Press. Best technique if you have a stronger upper body than your opposite number. Keep your arm close to your body and use wrist pressure to manoeuvre your opponent's hand so that his palm is facing the ceiling with your hand on top. Then force his arm down using your shoulder and triceps strength.

Top roll. With this move you're using guile, not muscle. At the start of the match, spread his fingers wide and attempt to open out his hand. Wiggle your hand out of his grip, walking your fingers to the edge of his hand – the closer to his fingertips the better. His hand should be wrapped around your wrist and your hand should be sticking out the top of his – similar to when your girlfriend refuses to hold your hand properly because you wouldn't wait for her hair straighteners to heat up. At this point push against his hand and while he's attempting to regain his grip, nail the match.

Advanced tips:

*   If you're competing in a tournament, vary your tactics – this will rest certain muscles between rounds and also confuse your opposition.

*   Shake hands with your opponent before the match to gauge how strong they are.

*   Try to prevent your wrist from being bent backwards. It is harder to win from this position.

*   Don't twist your shoulder and look away from the table. Keep your head and shoulders facing forward and pivot round by exerting pressure from the whole of your upper body.

*   Look your opponent in the eye and smile. Blowing kisses is probably a bit OTT though.

Know your beef

Used to eating our beef in minced form between two hamburger buns, few of us actually know one end of a cow from the other or would even recognize a piece of chuck if it hit us in the face. And that can be problematic when in the queue at the butcher's getting the shopping for your lady or mum.

Here's how to tell your rump from your ribeye and your chuck from your clod – and how to cook them when you get home:

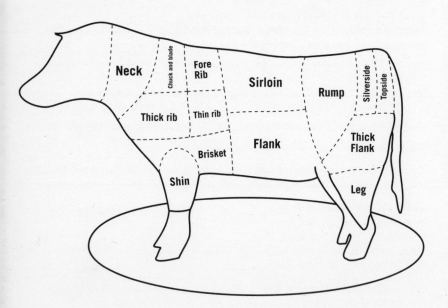

Neck or clod. Often simply called 'stewing' steak. Use for stews and braising as needs long slow cooking.

Chuck. Also called 'chine'. For braising, stewing and in pie fillings.

Blade. The shoulder meat. Good for braising and long cooking as the meat is nicely marbled with fat and will flavour and moisten the dish as it cooks. Perfect for boeuf bourguignon.

Ribeye/fore rib. Very tender rib meat – pan frying, grilling or sautéing single steaks, roasting for racks or joints.

T-bone steak. Large T-shaped steak combining the lower end of the sirloin and fillet steak.

Fillet steak. From the loin or centre of the back of the cow. Extremely lean and tender. Grill or fry.

Thin rib. The slices between the bones are entrecote steaks – roast, grill or fry.

Brisket. Is sometimes sold rolled for a slow or pot roast. Also used for stewing, braising and salting, for example in pastrami.

Tip:
To braise a piece of meat, first seal it off in a very hot pan for thirty seconds or so on each side. Then add cooking liquid to the pot – beer, wine, stock, etc. – and cook on a very low simmer until the meat is tender and easily torn apart with a fork.

Shin. From the foreleg of the cow. Needs very long, slow cooking. The gelatinous quality of this cut will thicken and flavour the sauce, so good for brawn, pies and steak puddings. Veal shin is used for the classic Italian dish *osso buco*.

Sirloin. The classic British steak. Can be fried, grilled or large sirloin cuts can be roasted.

Flank. Slightly fattier meat. For stewing, braising and for mince.

Rump. A top-quality meat for frying, grilling or roasting as a large piece.

Silverside. Slow roasting or a top-quality braising steak.

Topside. A roasting joint, topside beef is very lean and fine textured. Needs extra fat around it when roasting to stop it becoming dry.

Thick flank. Like topside and silverside, better braised than roasted to prevent this lean meat from becoming dry and stringy.

Leg. From the hind leg. As for shin, needs long slow cooking.

How to score a strike in ten-pin bowling

The ten-pin bowling shoe. With seams as thick as a Cornish pasty crimp and leather as shiny as a disco ball, no self-respecting gent would be seen dead wearing a pair outside the bowling alley.

Here's how to make sure your strikes get all the stares instead:

Step 1. Pick up your ball with both hands and rest the weight in your left hand. Place your thumb in the biggest hole, lay your palm flat against the surface of the ball, and slot your middle fingers, not your index finger, in the two remaining holes. Your choices of grip are:

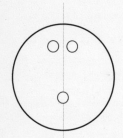

Conventional grip – more purchase on the ball, best for beginners.

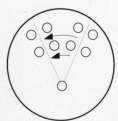
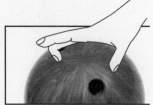

Fingertip grip – more scope for the hook ball.

Step 2. Start your approach four steps back from the foul line and slightly to the right of centre. Lift the ball to your chin, with your thumb pointing towards your face, and stare down the pins over the ball.

Step 3. Keep your shoulders and hips square to the foul line and step forward with your right foot. Simultaneously push the ball out the length of your arm. Keep your arm straight and let it swing back naturally with the weight of the ball.

Step 4. By the third step the ball should be behind you and your knees bent slightly.

Step 5. As the tip of your left foot lands near the foul line the ball should have swung back in the same arc and you can release. Try to release the ball onto the polished wooden floor in a fluid motion so it glides along the surface; don't throw it.

Step 6. The follow-through should see your arm up in front of your face and your right leg off at an angle like a ballerina.

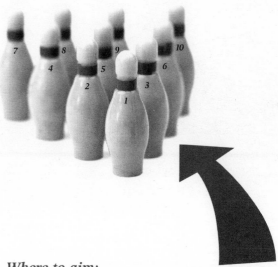

Where to aim:

To score a strike you need to aim at the 'pocket' – the space between pin 1 and 3. By knocking pin 1 over, the ball will crash into 3 and fly through to pin 5 before smashing into pin 9. Hitting the pocket maximizes internal pyramid damage and picks off the periphery pins, sending your skittles to the great big bowling alley in the sky.

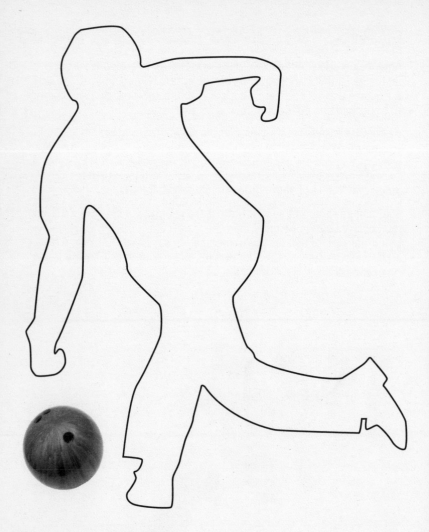

Mastering the hook ball:

Hook balls curve the path of the ball giving you more chance of hitting the pocket. Use a fingertip grip so your thumb is released first. This disrupts the stability of the ball as your fingers come out a little later, coupled with twisting or rolling your wrist from left to right the spin on the ball will cause it to curve or arc towards the pocket.

How to choose a bowling ball:

American men keep their own balls wrapped up in cotton wool and secured in a large leather handbag. Brits on the other hand coolly grab the first one they come across, not realizing it's a 16lb electric-blue-monstrosity that will put their shoulder out of joint after two throws.

Heavier balls knock more pins over, but lighter balls are more accurate. Try several balls for weight and size. As a rule, you should opt for the heaviest ball you are comfortable with, but remember you'll be swinging it several times so don't hit above your weight or your arm will get tired very quickly.

Your fingers should fit snugly, but not too snugly, and the space between the holes should be no more than the length of your palm. Once you've found the perfect ball for you, remember it, and use it every time. Balls will usually be colour coded for weight, and they also will have a serial number on them.

A 12lb ball is perfect for a ten-pin virgin.

Blagger's guide to playing rugby league

A worldwide winter sport, the gentleman's game complements the cold snap of the westerly winds with biting tackles and ice-cool runs. But the arrival of a searing sun doesn't mean the oval balls have to be relegated to the changing room. Find a clearing on a sandy beach or soft grassy field and you've got yourself a pitch. Follow these quick, rough-around-the-edges (and somewhat improvised) rules and you've got yourself a game.

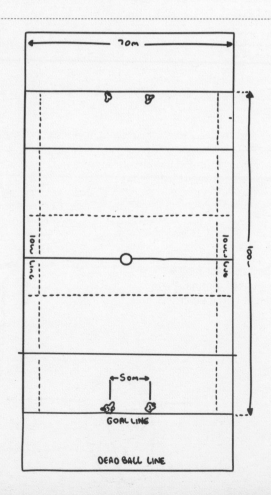

* Separate the teams evenly and mark out the playing field's parameters (including a halfway line) with scores in the sand or with jumpers.

* Flip a coin. With the rest of his team behind him, the loser of the toss-up kicks to the opposing team from the halfway line. This is also the procedure from a restart – the team that conceded the try must kick to the scoring team.

* When in possession always pass backwards and, whenever you're tackled, hit the deck. When tackling, be sure to ground the player and then release and allow them to roll the ball back between their legs to a fellow teammate.

* Possession switches to the other team when the ball is lost in contact, kicked under pressure or put down for a try over the line.

* The ball also gets turned over (i.e possession switches to opposite side) after six consecutive tackles.

* Penalties are not awarded due to the absence of a referee. However, ungentlemanly conduct can be punished with a wedgie.

* To make things easier, lineouts become simple uncontested throw-ins and, for the purpose of these rules, scrums are left to the Lions team.

* Conversions are also obsolete owing to a lack of goalposts.
A tall friend standing with his arms held out like a human Y will be a worthy substitute,but he'll probably get a broken nose and a mouthful of rugby ball for his troubles.

* Tactics: stay in a line, shuffle the pack with varying lengths
of passing and make the ball do
the work.

* After this punishing workout,
you'll need a drink. Head
straight to the nearest boozer
for a pint.

What to look for when you buy your first second-hand car

Cars are like children. You clean them, look after them and even christen them. Unlike children, you can also buy and sell them, and most of the time they do what they are told.

Here's how to choose a used motor that won't misbehave like a toddler after two cans of cola:

☐ Check the exterior of the car thoroughly. Walking around with a clipboard and checklist is probably going too far, but look for any recently done paintwork or dents that could knock a small amount of money off the asking price.

☐ The tyres should have good tread depth, with no bald patches or bulges.

☐ Check for rust damage – the wheel arches are particularly susceptible so get down on your hunkers and get a good look.

☐ Inspect the interior for tears, rips and scratches and make sure the mileage corresponds with the car's condition. If there's low mileage but the steering wheel is shiny and the foot pedals are worn, the car has probably done more miles than David Coulthard.

☐ Ensure there's a substantial amount of time to run on the MOT certificate and that there is a V5 logbook. If there isn't a logbook, don't buy the car. Without the V5 logbook the car's history cannot be checked and the car could be stolen, cloned or a cut-and-shut (when two different cars are welded together) – which all amount to you buying a car you won't actually legally own.

☐ HPI checks are a useful way of checking a car's financial and document history. They're available online for up to £20. All you have to do is enter the car's registration and you'll find out whether there is outstanding finance – money still owed to the company the seller bought it off – as well as any serious previous damage the seller may not have notified you of. If the car was a previous write-off – declared a 'total loss' by insurers after an accident – it may have previously been beyond repair. HPI will tell you if it's still legitimately roadworthy.

☐ Finally, if everything's in order take your new baby for a test spin. If the driving glove fits, pay the man his money, shake his hand and pray the wheels don't fall off at the bottom of the drive.

Advanced tip:

Join the AA or a similar organization if you need a second opinion before buying – they will send someone to assess the car you have your eye on.

o   As good as new
o   Only one previous owner
o   Low Mileage

Essential painting and decorating tips

Michelangelo. Painter. Sculptor. Teenage Mutant Ninja Turtle. The ultimate Renaissance man. The ceiling of the Sistine Chapel – his greatest achievement – took him four years to complete, the time it will take you to decorate your living room if you're going it alone. From stripping to cutting in, here's the idiot's guide to decorating from scratch.

Your tools:

Buy your tools from a good trade counter – pay by cash and buy in bulk and you can expect a good discount.

Good quality paint brushes. Buy the best quality brush that you can afford. Pure bristle brushes (horse and Chinese boar) are considered best quality, give a good finish and will last a long time if looked after.

Paint rollers. Choose lambskin, mohair or synthetic rather than foam which gives an uneven finish. **NB: The smoother the surface, the shorter the pile of roller.**

* use a short ½" pile for applying emulsion to fresh plaster or flat walls and ceilings.

* use a ¼" nap for glossy walls.

* use a medium ½" pile for textured or uneven surfaces such as woodchip and on ceilings.

* use a long pile head for embossed papers and bare brickwork.

You will also need:

* Paint tray.

* Coarse sandpaper.

* Sugar soap and sponge.

*   Stepladder.

*   Dustsheets and tarpaulin – old bed sheets work well.

*   Rags for wiping.

*   Masking and duct tape.

*   White spirit.

Decorating tips:

*   Use one dominant colour in flat and emulsion paint for the main walls, another for the ceiling and use a gloss colour, usually white, for the window frames and skirting board.

*   **Light colours make a room look bigger and – you guessed it – dark colours make a room look smaller. Painting the ceiling white will make it appear higher.**

*   Use a strong, statement colour to paint one contrasting wall in a large room for a dramatic effect.

*   Take photographs of the room and adjust the wall colour in Photoshop.

*   If you're painting over a darker colour with a lighter one, use primer and leave for a day before painting in your main colour.

> **Advanced tips:**
>
> Keep a wet cloth in your pocket to deal with any lumps of paint or dirt on the wall.
>
> To remove vertical roll marks, roll over them horizontally within ten minutes.
>
> Apply a second coat if you can still see the previous colour underneath.

*   Estimate the amount of paint you'll need. As a general rule, one gallon of paint covers between 150 and 300 square feet of wall. However, to make sure you don't go over budget, or run out of paint, measure the height and width of the walls you're painting and round them up. There are many free paint coverage calculators available online and once you put in the measurements you'll be told how much paint you'll need to get the job done.

Always buy one extra can of paint, you don't want to get towards the end of the job and have to nip out for some more.

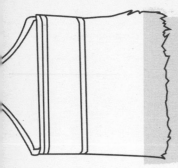

You will need at least three brushes:

½" *brush* – for very tight areas and window frames

1" and 1½" – use for 'cutting in', i.e. painting round fiddly edges of walls before painting large areas with roller or brush, and for doorframes and small and hard-to-reach areas

How to prepare a room for decoration:

1. Stare at the wall for several minutes, shaking your head and tutting. Clap your hands together loudly. Well done. You've earned your first tea break.

2. Remove shelves, mirrors and hooks from the wall. Wrap light fixtures with black bin liners and seal the top with a wrap of duct tape.

3. Remove any chipped paint and sand smooth before painting over.

4. Dust off the walls and ceiling, then clean with warm soapy water – work from the bottom up to stop streaks of dirt marking the wall. For very dirty walls and windows in kitchens, use a sugar soap solution to remove all grease before painting.

5. Remove any mould or mildew with a 50% water, 50% bleach solution. Wear rubber gloves and scrub the wall clean. Rinse with cold water.

6. Cover carpets and flooring with tarpaulin. Tape the edges and make sure there are no bubbles or creases, as this will allow paint to seep through.

7. Move all furniture into the centre of the room and cover with dustsheets.

8. Windows should be shut, but keep the room ventilated with a fan.

9. Fill in any nail holes with filler, smooth over and let dry for two hours. Sand off the top and paint the patch of wall with primer.

10. Use masking tape to mark off the edges of the ceiling and on light switches and windows to give a clean, sharp edge and avoid smearing.

11. One lump or two? Time for another tea break.

2" – for cutting in walls before painting with roller and painting doors and skirting boards

3", 4" and 5" – ideal for large areas and large expanses of woodwork

Always flick new brushes across your hand a few times to remove loose hairs.

Painting tips:

The correct order for painting a room is ceiling, walls and lastly, woodwork. Always try to finish an entire wall or area in one go – a half-finished wall will leave a drying mark which will remain visible on the finished surface.

1. Always read the paint instructions carefully. Shake the tin, open and stir. Pour a quarter of the paint into the tray or holder; never dip a brush or roller straight into the tin.

2. Cut in. Use the smaller brush to paint a border of a couple of inches at the edges of the walls and around any taped fixtures. Don't leave jagged marks, keep vertically or horizontally in line with the wall.

3. When using the roller, roll it several times in the tray to load it evenly on the roller. Don't overload it with paint. When painting, use a sweeping stroke, and start a foot from the edge and bottom of the wall. With only a little pressure – any more could damage the rolling cloth – roll upwards at a slight angle and paint a capital W on the wall, stopping a couple of inches from the ceiling. Fill in the spaces in-between with gentle up and down brush strokes.

4. Spread the paint you've just applied by gently rolling over it.

5. Always leave a wet edge. By painting on top of a wet edge you won't see any overlapping marks. Repeat until the entire wall is coated.

6. Never leave the edges to dry, so always complete a wall before taking a break.

7. Once finished, roll up and down over the whole wall without any paint on your roller – get as close to the edges as possible but don't allow the roller to touch them. This will blend the layer of paint smoothly.

8. For the ceiling, work away from the window and work across the width of the ceiling in wide 1m bands. Reapply paint at the beginning of each new band.

9. Leave the paint to dry for 24 hours, then remove all the masking tape by pulling it off gently at a 90° angle.

Stand back and take in your handiwork.

How to clean your roller and brushes:

For water-based emulsions, clean immediately under cold running water until all traces are removed. Hot water can damage some brushes. For oil-based paints, clean immediately with white spirit to remove all paint then wash in warm soapy water. For latex paint, run under warm water until all flecks of paint are gone.

Scrape any excess paint from rollers with an old kitchen knife. Wash with warm water and detergent, scrub away with your fingers and rinse until the water runs clear.

Resist the temptation to soak your brushes in a bucket of water; the wood will expand, then shrink. This leaves the metal casing enlarged and results in loose bristles.

Allow the brushes to dry completely, straighten out the bristles and store in a brush keeper or hang upside down. Don't keep bristles down in a jam jar as this bends the bristles.

Saving money on car maintenance

Make sure the rubber on the wiper blades isn't splitting; the exposed metal could scratch your windscreen and you'll need to fork out for a new one.

The correct tyre pressure is important. Check your handbook, or there are often stickers on the doorframe. Alternatively, most petrol stations have a sign on the wall telling you each car make's tyre pressure. Keep your tyres at the right pressure and you'll use less fuel.

In winter, mix antifreeze with the water in the windscreen washers – 25% antifreeze to 75% water dilution, roughly – and frequently check the engine's water in the summer months.

Wash the wheel arches with a pressure washer, as this will prevent the build-up of mud which attracts moisture and cause rust.

Most car manufacturers recommend getting a service every 15,000 miles. And after every new set of tyres get a wheel alignment check so they'll wear evenly and last longer.

You also need to get a new cam belt about every 70,000 miles, so keep an eye on the mileage counter.

The little dents in the tyre, the tread, should be 1.6 millimetres deep. You can check this by getting a 10 pence piece and putting it sideways on in the tread. The tread should cover the edge of the coin to a depth covering the circumference of the coin as shown. If not you could be liable to a fine of £1,000 and points on your licence.

1.6mm

Finally, remember to check your oil regularly. Park on a flat service, pull the dipstick out, wipe it clean, put it back in and pull it back out again to see what the level is. There are lines showing min and max; it should always be just below max.

How to organize a stag do like the best best man in history

Bells chime in the background, glorious sunshine filters through the church's arching doorway as you walk down the aisle sharing nods and checking your pockets for the ring. Your clammy hands search your waistcoat, your fingertips pre-empting the warm halo of gold imprinted against your chest. Damn. You've left it on the bed stand. Best man becomes worst man. Here's how to nail the stag do at least.

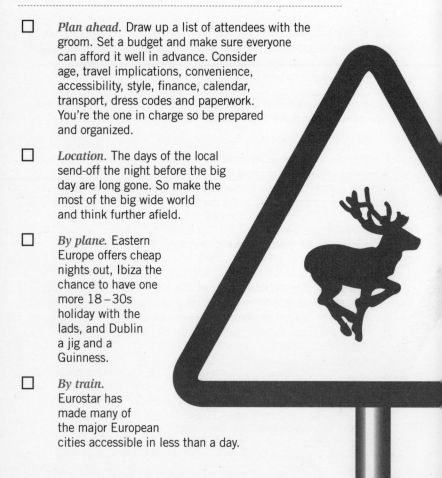

- ☐ *Plan ahead.* Draw up a list of attendees with the groom. Set a budget and make sure everyone can afford it well in advance. Consider age, travel implications, convenience, accessibility, style, finance, calendar, transport, dress codes and paperwork. You're the one in charge so be prepared and organized.

- ☐ *Location.* The days of the local send-off the night before the big day are long gone. So make the most of the big wide world and think further afield.

- ☐ *By plane.* Eastern Europe offers cheap nights out, Ibiza the chance to have one more 18–30s holiday with the lads, and Dublin a jig and a Guinness.

- ☐ *By train.* Eurostar has made many of the major European cities accessible in less than a day.

Daytime:	Evening:
• 4x4 Off-Roading	• Burlesque Cabaret Night
• Brewery Tour	• Lap-Dancing Club
• Clay-Pigeon Shooting	• Comedy Club
• Kite Buggying	• Fancy-Dress Pub Crawl – dress up and hit the locals
• Sky Dive	• Greyhound Races
• Golf	• Beach Party
• Go-Karting	• An Ice Bar
• Archery	
• Paintballing	

☐ *By automobile.* From the bustling capitals of Cardiff, Edinburgh, Belfast and London to the recently rejuvenated inner sanctums of Bristol, Portsmouth, Liverpool and Newcastle, cities are a stag's best friend.

☐ *Or if you prefer the open spaces.* A surfing weekend in Cornwall or a camping and fishing holiday in Scotland

☐ *Daytime activities.* You need to have activities prepared for the day because drinking for twenty-four hours straight will result in liver disease; not the best send-off for your best mate. Sporting or outdoor activities make drinking all day virtually impossible and furnish conversation for the evening; especially if some of the invited either don't know and/or hate each other.

☐ *Evening activities.* In the evening, book a restaurant and then after-dinner entertainment. Many venues don't accept stag dos so ring ahead and check, and if you're going to turn up dressed as vicars and nuns make sure the staff know what to expect and don't turn you away mistaking you for the inebriated Christian Convention party they had in the week before.

One more word of warning, if the stag party is staying away overnight, book accommodation in advance and try not to arrive at the hotel too outrageously drunk: you might be turned away and tied to a lamppost naked instead of the groom-to-be.

Blagger's guide to horse racing

The office trip to the races. A confusing, drunken affair that's never complete until you've lost your month's wages and won a hangover. Here's how to make sure you don't place all your hard-earned cash on a 'night-mare'.

Racing terms to bandy about:

Furlong. The length of a race is measured in furlongs. One mile equals eight furlongs. The shortest races are run over five furlongs. The longest, the Grand National, is run over four and a half miles (7.2km).

Pace. The speed set by the leading horses at the start and the middle of the race.

Blown up. When a horse begins to wane during a race.

Length. The length of a horse, used when describing the distances between horses during the race and at the finishing line.

Winning by a short head or a distance. A short head is minimal whereas a distance is up to 30 lengths or so.

Hacked up. Used when a horse wins easily.

Penalty. A weight added to a horse to even out the chances. Weights are allocated according to past performance in handicapped races.

Pulling. Horse that is using energy fighting with the jockey rather than running to win.

Stayers. Horses with good stamina and therefore better for longer races and heavy-going conditions.

Other racing terms:

The 'going'. The condition of the course. Some horses perform better on firm courses, while others thrive on soft or muddy courses. Depending on the condition on the race day, the going is classified as either hard, firm, good to firm, good, good to soft, soft or heavy.

Claiming race. A race where horses are entered for a certain amount of money to ensure no amateurs take part.

Handicap. Race where penalty weights are placed on horses running.

Sprint. Race of seven furlongs or less.

Steeplechase. Race with fences and water hazards.

National hunt. Race with hurdles and fences. August – May traditionally. Unusual to be run on all-weather surfaces.

Flat. Normally summer but can be all year round – run on all-weather surfaces.

Maiden race. The runners are all horses that have never won a race.

Colt. Male horse four years old or younger.

Filly. Female horse four years old or younger.

Rabbit. Horse which is entered in a race to set a fast pace but won't last the distance.

Claimer. Apprentice flat race jockey.

Apprentice. Young jockey with a trainer.

Understanding how to read the race card will help you make an informed guess on which horse to bet on. It gives information on the horse, its age and any penalty weight it will carry in the race. Also listed are the rider, the trainer and the owner's name, and, most importantly, codes which give information on how the horse has performed in recent races, or its 'form'.

* Time, name and distance of race.

* Prize money – this is split between the jockey, owner and trainer. Prize money is also awarded to horses in second or third place.

* Horse name – punters with less experience, often place a bet on a horse with a name they fancy. The country the horse comes from may be in brackets after the name.

* Horse number – the number the jockey will wear on his back. The number in brackets is the stall the horse will start from.

* Owner – the owner's name. Certain owners will have good form.

* Trainer – the trainer will know his horse inside out and monitor their form. Their job is to work with the jockey, gauge the weather and running, and get the horse in top form and condition for the race. Punters should follow the form of the trainer and jockey.

* Name of jockey – often a crucial element in the outcome of a race. Trainers will often stick to a known combination of horse and a rider who knows that horse well.

* Age of horse – flat races are normally run by younger horses. Certain races such as the Derby are only open to three-year-olds. The Grand National is only open to horses over five years old.

* Weight allowance – the weight, including the jockey, which the horse must carry. Jockeys must weigh in before the race and are often on diets to keep their ideal weight. Flat race jockeys are usually much smaller and lighter than jump jockeys.

* Jockey's colours – the rider's silks, or the coloured top he wears, are crucial when following the race. Outlandish silk shirts include spots, stripes, diamonds and stars.

* Number of days since the horse last ran a competitive race – indicated by the number after the horse's name. The higher the number the lower the race fitness of the horse.

> **Odds can be long or short**
>
> *200-1* are long odds and mean the horse is less likely to come in winner.
>
> *2-1* are short odds and indicative of a potential winner or at least a good place.
>
> *Odds on* (favourite)– where the odds are less than evens or less than 2.0 decimal

09.09.09

RACECARD

2.00 Wilkinson Frenchgate Nursery (Class 3)
For 2yo Rated 0-95 Weights highest weight not less than 9st 7lb Weights raised 4lb Minimum weight 7-12 Penalties after August 29th, each race won 6lb Penalty value 1st £9.714 2nd £2,890.50 3rd £1,444.50 4th £721.50

£15,000 guaranteed

7f
GD-FM

No.		Form	Horse, breeding, owner		Wgt	Jockey/trainer	OR	TS	RPR
1 (9)		11	**MR GRINCH** 12 b g Green Tune - Flyamore M J K Dods	2	9-7	Phillip Makin M Dods	90	82	97
2 (5)		004016	**DESERT AUCTION** 19 D b c Desert Style - Double Gamble A J Ilsley, K T Ivory & G Battocchi	2	9-6	Steve Drowne R Hannon	89	92	95
3 (1)		34211	**LUCKY RAVE** 13 D b c Lucky Story - Rave On Ron Hull	2	9-5	D Brown	88	79	**98**
4 (3)		231847	**FARMER GILES** 21 b c Danroad - Demeter R A Green	2	9-2	T P Queally M Bell	85	96	96
5 (12)		219	**ATACAMA CROSSING** 33 b c Footstepsinthesand - Endure Paul Moulton	2	9-0	T P O'Shea B Hills	83	85	91
6 (6)		071	**PLEASANT DAY** 20 D b g Noverre - Sunblush Jaber Abdullah	2	8-13b	L Dettori B Meehan	82	66	94
7 (7)		3128	**AUDACITY OF HOPE** 18 b c Red Ransom - Aliena Four Winds Racing	2	8-13t	K Fallon P McBride	82	93	9
8 (8)		91	**BRICK RED** 16 ch c Dubawi - Duchcov Brick Racing	2	8-11	William Buick A Balding	80	75	
9 (13)		4616	**JUTLAND** 18 D BF b c Halling - Dramatique Sheikh Hamdan Bin Mohammed Al Maktoum	2	8-8	Greg Fairley M Johnston	77	90	
10 (10)		533120	**FLANEUR** 22 b c Chineur - Tatanka Jeremy Gompertz	2	8-8b	David Allan T Easterby	77	**97**	
11 (4)		415	**MISS SMILLA** 46 b f Red Ransom - Snowing Findlay & Bloom	2	8-8	Tony Culhane K Ryan	77	8	
12 (2)		233012	**TRANSFIXED** 19 D b f Trans Island - Rectify Mrs I M Folkes	2	8-7	John Egan P Evans	76	9	
		01	**RANSOM NOTE** 18 D b c Red Ransom - Zacheta	2	8-6	Michael Hills B Hills	61	75	

Jamie Spenc

Brick Red 12/1 Atacama

Reading the form:

/	the horse did not run in the last season
–	the dash separates the current season from the last. The position form is read from right to left, e.g. 0-135 – horse finished 5th in last race, 3rd in race before that, 1st in one before that, and the previous season placed outside the top nine.

P or PU	horse pulled up and didn't finish race
F	fallen
B or BD	brought down
U	unseated rider
RTR	refused to race
RO	ran out

C	won on today's course
D	won on today's distance
CD	won on both course and distance
BF	in last race this horse was the beaten favourite
RPR	Racing Post rating
TS	top speed
OR	official rating as compiled by the British Horse Racing Board (BHB)

Types of bet:

Simple odds. 6/1 said 'six to one' means you'll make a profit of six pounds for every pound you bet. You also get back your stake so you'd win £7. Betting will change throughout a race and the final bet is the bet you win on. Bets can be locked if you tell the bookie you'll have the current price when you place your bet.

To win. Also referred to as 'on the nose' – means a bet on a selected horse to win overall.

The place. Only available at the racecourse, these winnings are only a fraction of the win price. You can choose a horse to be placed and therefore your horse should finish in the top three. In a race of 5–7 horses you must be placed first or second. For a race with 1–4 you cannot have a placed bet. In a handicapped race of up to 16 horses you can be placed 1–4. A place bet only gives you $\frac{1}{4}$ or $\frac{1}{5}$ of the usual odds win.

Each way bet. Two bets in one; a win bet and a place bet. If your horse wins you get both bets back but if it only places you receive the return from only the place bet. For example, if you put £2 – which would actually cost you £4 because it's a two bets in one deal – on each way for a horse at 4-1 and your horse wins, you'll get back £8 in return plus your £2 original stake, £2 for a quarter of the odds and £2 for the place bet stake.

Straight forecast. You must select the first and second places in a series of races. Also called an Exacta bet. More common in greyhound racing.

The place pot. UK tote bet in which you must bet on a horse being placed in the first six races of any meet.

Accumulator. Also known as a 'roll-up' – is one bet with four or more selections from different races. All your selected horses must win in order to make a return. Wins from each selection are accumulated or reinvested on the successive races.

Each-way accumulator. As above but with two bets on four or more selections in different races. The first bet is on horses to win, and the second bet on horses to be placed.

The scoop 6. For TV viewers only, often on a Saturday. Bet on the winners of six selected TV races.

The Horserace Totalizator Board, the Tote, was created by Parliament in 1928 and the first board was set up by Winston Churchill with the aim of providing a safe, government-controlled alternative to illegal bookmakers. Branded Totesport, the Tote owns over 500 betting shops and has over 60 outlets on British racecourses. They are the only organization in the UK allowed to run pool betting on horse racing.

How to place a bet at the bookies

Entering a bookies for the first time can be a potentially embarrassing experience if you haven't a clue what you are doing and it's full of hardened punters shouting at the screens. So here's a quick idiot's guide.

* Pick up a slip and look at the screens. All the information you need is shown on them – from events to odds.

* The betting odds represent the probability of the outcome of the event if the event was repeated over and over. Write in your stake, for example £3. Your selection (or horse's name), the time of race, e.g. 3.15. And finally the course, for example Ascot.

* Take the slip to the counter. Your details will be processed and you will be given a receipt.

* Make sure you say, 'I'll take the price please' as this will guarantee you receive the odds on your slip. They will confirm this by writing it on the slip. Until you get the hang of the betting lark, always take the current price as the odds normally shorten throughout the day.

* Now all you have to do is to wait for your horse to come in and book a flight to Las Vegas. Where you can lose it all at leisure...

Further hints and tips for the novice:

* Avoid apprentice and maiden races – quite simply they're harder to predict because if a horse has never won a race before it makes it harder to judge the odds.

* All-weather races should be avoided until you know several horses and jockeys well enough to gauge a win or a place.

* A long gap since the horse's last outing could mean it isn't fit or it's been held back for a possible win in a major race.

* Study the form. Learn everything you can about the horse, jockey and trainer you want to back.

* The draw, or the horse's placing in the starting stalls in flat races, can affect how a horse runs. Find out what different courses' draws mean to the outcome

* How your horse reacts to jumps over different heights is important when choosing who to back in a National Hunt. Again, try to find out more about its form over jumps; some courses are more difficult so horses need to be experienced.

* Balance youth and experience when picking a horse to bet on.

* *The Racing Post* is a good place to begin when trying to understand the complex language of horse racing. And even if you can't read a word of it at first, waltzing around the track with a copy under your arm will make you look like a true punter.

How to moonwalk like Michael Jackson

When you add up all of Michael Jackson's hit songs from 'ABC' to 'Billie Jean' – let's forget 'Heal the World' for now – not to mention all his groundbreaking albums – it's quite easy to forget the dancing legacy he also left behind.

In honour of the late and great Jacko here's how to pay homage to a musical legend:

Step 1. Slide your feet into some slip-ons without much grip on the sole; a pair of your dad's slippers will do the trick.

Step 2. Pull on one white glove.

Step 3. Find a shiny wooden or tile floor on an even surface.

Step 4. Place your feet about a foot apart with your left foot at the front.

Step 5. Lift your right heel and place your weight on your right toes. Bend your right knee slightly to help with balance. Your sole should be at a right angle to the floor.

Step 6. Keeping your left foot flat and your leg straight, slide it back across the floor.

Step 7. Once your left foot is a foot behind your right foot, straighten your right leg and snap your right heel down. Simultaneously raise your left heel, by bending your knee, and shift your weight over to your left toe. Important: both toes never leave the floor.

Step 8. Slide your right foot back and keep it flat to the floor. If you want to add another layer of coolness, as you slide your left foot back move your right arm forward and vice versa.

Step 9. Repeat the movements.

Step 10. Show off your moonwalking skills during drunken nights out, children's parties and weddings.

How to get off the phone from a cold caller

The four horsemen of the apocalypse. War, Famine, Death and Cold Callers. Drastic telecom times call for drastic telecom measures.

The softly-softly approach. Wait for the salesperson to finish and then calmly tell them you're sorry but you're not interested. If they keep on at you – which they usually do – tell them you've complained to the police regarding cold caller harassment. Ask for their company number and individual name and once they freak out they'll say their goodbyes and leave you in peace.

Time on your side? Pretend to listen attentively to what they're telling you and feign an interest in their product. Answer all their questions and then at the all-important moment of payment inform them you don't a) have the money, b) have any means of paying over the phone, and c) understand the payment system.

Reverse the roles. Ask the cold caller to participate in your very own Cold Caller Questionnaire. 'It should only take about an hour, are you interested?' The chances are they won't be.

Bamboozle them to death. No matter what they're selling, ask intricate and incredibly specific questions. This can cause havoc for the script-reading slaves. If they're selling you a washing machine ask them if it can get bloodstains out or if the outlet tube will take a Q46 tubular bell designed by Mike Oldfield in 1846. Bamboozle and bugger about. They'll eventually admit defeat. After all, time is money and money is what makes the telecom occult tick.

Play with their heads. A cruel option but an option nonetheless. On answering, say you're not the right person to talk to and place the receiver on the worktop. Once the muffled 'Hellos' die down they'll have finally got the hint and hung up. Alternatively, pick up the phone and say 'Hello.' When they begin to speak say, 'Hello? Is anyone there? Hello?' Wait a few more minutes and repeat. Soon enough you'll hear the sweet sound of a cold caller flat-lining.

How to get served at a busy bar

In France they drink demis of lager. We drink pints. In France they are waited on by polite waiters. In Britain we have to survive a primeval scrum in order to get our mitts on a beer. In France committing a crime of passion can result in a lighter jail sentence. In Britain there is no such thing. But what could be a more passionate affair than that of a Brit and his beer? Judicial difference aside, there is a formula for getting served at a busy bar.

The first thing to do is find the least busy part of the bar, away from the pumps. Situate yourself behind someone who's being served and as they turn and leave, shoot your arm through, grab onto the bar counter, and pull yourself through the gap. Next, gently ease your shoulders into the gap, squeezing any others out of the way, so you are standing facing the bar. Now, get the barman's attention. Don't shout like you're head's on fire, just be patient and concentrate. Don't get distracted in conversation with the mate who is helping you carry the drinks – stay focused or you may miss your chance. A moment will arise when the barman finishes serving someone and looks up for his next customer, that's the moment you strike. Even if you know that the person next to you has been waiting for ages, when the barman asks 'Who's next', never hesitate. Get in there and take no prisoners! With a big smile on your face, raise your eyebrows and make eye contact. Once you have their precious attention, give him or her your order in a clear and friendly voice. Soon enough you'll be supping your nice cold beer safe in the knowledge you didn't have to kill anyone to get it.

Advanced tips:

Shorten the odds. Work in pairs. If two of you go to different areas of the bar, you double your chances of being served. Stay in constant eye contact. The first one to get to the barman orders for both of you. Use your charm. If there is a female bartender, a surefire tip is to say loudly to a female customer near you that she is next. You will be served immediately after.

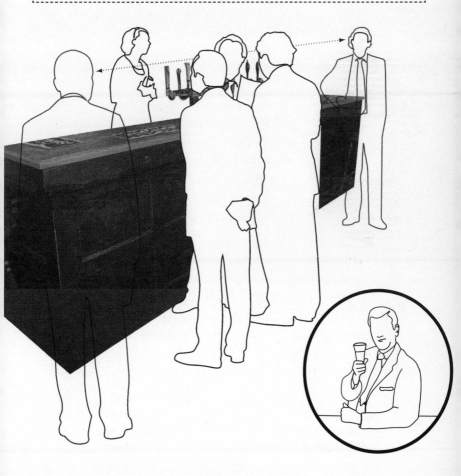

How to put up shelves *like a superhero*

You will need:

- brackets
- AC electrical detector
- pipe detector
- screwdriver
- electric drill with masonry bit
- hammer
- screws (50mm or longer)
- Rawlplugs (at least 30mm)
- pencil
- spirit level.

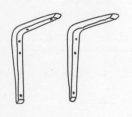

Hollywood's new forte for retelling fairy tales with a modern-day twist isn't as popular this side of the pond. We British like our stories a little dog-eared, a little worn by the winds of time. We prefer a little dirt to a little shine. Just look at EastEnders. Our cultural diet is low in drama because we get our fill from other quarters. Quarters less glamorous than the star-sprinkled studios and red carpets. Let's face it; the British can make a trip to B&Q as explosive as all four Die Hards *rolled into one. From wonky trolley wheels to tumbling timber, DIY is the Disney of our nation.*

After the midday match and before the Saturday night steak, the quest for the Excalibur of the toolbox must begin. We wade into the treacherous garage, plunge our hand into the sea of dust, clutch the handle and pull, as if from stone, the drill which will lead the way in the almighty quest of putting up shelves.

1. First, run your AC electrical and pipe detector along the chosen wall. Depending on the model, it will flash or beep if there are any electrical cables or gas or water pipes behind the scenes. Once you've got the all-clear, place the shelf against the wall and mark its edges with your pencil. Don't stretch, use a ladder if need be.

2. Hold one bracket up, a few inches in from your original mark, place the spirit level on top of the bracket. Make sure the spirit bubble is roughly centred on the level and mark the position of the bracket's

holes. If you're putting up a floating shelf, the bracket will be one long frame the width of the shelf as opposed to two separate brackets placed at either end.

3.   If there is a lady in the house, it is worth asking her if she is entirely happy with the positioning of the shelf. She may have wanted it in the alcove, not above the fireplace, so consult at this point.

4.   Take the bracket away and use the electrical drill to make two pilot holes in the wall, using a masonry drill bit with a diameter slightly less than that of the holes in your bracket, but corresponding to the size of your Rawlplugs. Drill all the holes to the depth of the Rawlplug by marking the drill bit at the correct depth with a felt-tip pen. A great way to save on mess at this point is to Blu Tac an envelope on the skirting board under each hole – this will collect the crumbs of plaster and paint and reduce the clear-up time once you've finished.

5.   Next, tap a Rawlplug into each hole using the hammer.

6.   Place the bracket back over and screw the screws in until it is secure. But don't screw too tightly.

7.   Hold the other bracket in place and rest the shelf across both brackets.

8.   Place the spirit level on the shelf and adjust the trajectory of the left-hand bracket until the bubble is in the middle of the level.

9.   Once you're happy, dot a mark in the holes of the other bracket with your pencil.

10.   Take the shelf and level away and screw in the other bracket as before, not forgetting the Rawlplugs and starting with the lower hole.

11.   Check the spirit level again, and step back to see if the symmetry is correct.

12.   Tighten all four screws flush with the wall.

13.   Last but not least, vertically screw the shelf into the brackets – make sure your screws are no longer than the width of your shelf. Put a weight on top of the shelf so it stays put, and tighten the screws in underneath through the holes at the front and back of the bracket.

Your new display area is now ready to hold your prized Disney films and *Die Hard* box set.

How to act when you're in a posh restaurant for the first time

Eating together has always been important to society. The word companion comes from Latin. 'Com' means 'with' or 'together' and 'Panis' means 'food' or 'bread'. So we have always correlated eating with togetherness and companionship, a time to share ideas and thoughts.

But, if 'eating out' normally means a quickie kebab or a KFC, dining in a posh restaurant for the first time is likely to pose a few challenges. You want to be judged on your personality, not your manners, so don't let them let you down.

The Basics:

* A good way to avoid committing a humiliating faux pas is to take an elongated sip of water at the start of each phase of the meal and watch what someone else does first. Peeling prawns, tackling a greasy snail or supping soup is a lot easier to do when you've had your own private demonstration. (If your fellow diners are necking the water too, dig in before the food gets cold. They can only copy your mistakes!)

* In certain company, be careful of what you say. Don't get too involved or heated (so watch your drink).

* Wait for your guest and others to tuck in before you do.

* Never answer your mobile phone or start texting while you're dining.

* If you pour yourself a glass of water or wine, offer those within your reach some and pour it twisting the bottle up and away when the glass is half full. Swallow your food before drinking (and your drink before eating) and hold your wine glass at the stem.

* Never lift your bowl or plate to your mouth to lick it, or sup the contents.

* If you are having shellfish such as oysters, mussels, prawns or lobster, you will probably be given a small bowl of water with a slice of lemon in it. This is not for drinking. It is for rinsing your fingers, so don't slurp it.

* **Never whistle at a waiter or click your fingers to gain their attention.** Simply make eye contact with a passing waiter and raise your hand slightly or simply say 'Excuse me'. No matter how long you are ignored for, resist the temptation to stick out your foot and trip up the waiter. Unless you are dining alone.

* If you run out of wine feel free to turn the bottle upside down in the cooler, ensuring it's completely empty first of course.

* Your napkin will be within your place setting so don't pinch your neighbour's. Never tuck it into your collar. Place it on your lap and don't blow your nose with it or crumple it up and put it on the plate at the end of the meal. Fold it loosely and place it back on the table.

* Order extras like water or a basket of bread first, then your starter and your main. It is polite to let a lady order first and the person who is paying should go last. In most high-end establishments the waiter will go round the table once and take your starter and main at the same time. He will return to take your dessert and coffee or cheese orders.

* Tear your bread, don't cut it and transfer butter onto your bread plate not directly from dish to dough. Don't spread butter on your bread all at once. Tear a small piece off, add butter, and then eat.

* When you've finished eating, place your knife and fork close together on your plate – not on top of one another – and rotate them so their points face roughly at 10 o'clock. Never push your plate away from you.

BLAGGER'S GUIDE TO AN ITALIAN MENU:

L'antipasto – 'before the meal' nibbles such as bread or olives

Il primo – 'first course' or starter

Il secondo – 'second course' or main meal

Il contorno – side dish, in Italy this will normally be a salad

Il dolce – dessert

Il conto – the bill

Il servizio – service charge or suggested tip

Il coperto – cover charge

BLAGGER'S GUIDE TO A FRENCH MENU:

Le menu – set menu with a fixed price and three or five courses depending on how much you pay

A la carte – dishes ordered independently from the main menu

La carte des vins – wine list

Une dégustation – nope, not disgusting. This is the tasting menu; multiple dishes of bite-size meals

Apéritif – pre-dinner drink

Hors d'œuvres – appetizers such as olives or canapés

Entrée – starter

Plat principal – main course

Digestif – after-dinner drink. Those French love a tipple

La plat du jour – daily special

L'ardoise – the specials board

Gratuit or offert – indicates these tit-bits are free

Des cuisses de grenouille – should you wish to brave it, frog's legs

Know your place setting

Use the cutlery from the outside in. Your dessert fork and spoon can be found at the top of your place mat. Once an item of cutlery has been used it should not touch the table. If you leave your place, rest your knife on your plate at 4 o'clock, blade facing in, and your fork at 8 o'clock.

Your glass is on your right.

Your bread is on your left.

Wine glass (white)

Wine glass (red)

Water glass

Soup spoon

Dinner spoon

Dinner knife

Dessert spoon

Cake fork

Service plate

Bread knife

Bread plate

Dinner fork

Salad fork

Napkin

Blagger's guide to wine

Between the ages of ten and sixteen, drinking alcohol usually involves necking a bottle of cider on a park bench or dabbling in your parents' drinks cabinet. Post-sixteen, girls enter the fray and, once you start dining out instead of vomiting in the car park, it's learn-your-wine-time.

Match your food with a wine:

FOOD	RED	WHITE
Red Meat (beef, lamb, veal)	Cabernet Sauvignon	White Zinfandel (Rose)
	Rioja	
	Chianti	
	Shiraz	
	Pinot Noir	
	Zinfandel	
White Meat (chicken, pork)	Pinot Noir	Pinot Grigio
	Merlot	Sauvignon Blanc
		Chardonnay
		White Zinfandel
		Riesling
Seafood	Merlot	Chardonnay
		Sauvignon Blanc
		Pinot Grigio
Pasta or vegeterian meals	Merlot	Chardonnay
	Valpolicella	Soave
Hot and spicy	Zinfandel	Gewurtztraminer
		White Zinfandel
		Riesling
		Sauvignon Blanc

The most respected regional wines:

REGION	RED	WHITE
France	Cabernet Sauvignon	Pinot Grigio
	Merlot	Sauvignon Blanc
	Pinot Noir	Chardonnay
		Riesling
		Gewurtstraminer
Germany		Riesling
Italy	Chianti	Soave
	Valpolicella	
Spain	Rioja	
Australia	Shiraz	Chardonnay
	Merlot	Riesling
	Cabernet Sauvignon	
New Zealand	Pinot Noir	Chardonnay
	Merlot	Sauvignon Blanc
South Africa		Chardonnay
		Sauvignon Blanc
Chile	Cabernet Sauvignon	Chardonnay
	Shiraz	Sauvignon Blanc
	Merlot	
Argentina	Cabernet Sauvignon	
California	Zinfandel	White Zinfandel
	Pinot Noir	
	Merlot	
	Cabernet Sauvignon	

How to make a bed
like a nurse

*Remember when your nan tucked you into bed and it felt
as though you were wearing a strait-jacket; your breath
constricted, your arms pinned close to your sides ... Blankets
and eiderdowns may be a thing of the past, but a nicely
made bed is a welcome retreat at the end of a hard day.
Here's how to do it in less than five minutes.*

Change your sheets and duvet cover every two weeks.

Spread the new bottom sheet over the bed and pull the corners so
they overhang the mattress evenly. Smooth out the centre and tuck any
spare sheet tightly under the side of the mattress. Don't worry about
hospital corners.

Pillows and duvets should be plumped and aired every two weeks. If
possible, leave them out in the sunshine for the day to give them a
good airing. Sunshine will also help kill any germs. Stuff your pillows in
pillowcases and place at the head of the bed. The open side of the pillows
should face the edge.

Turn your duvet cover inside out. To save time, you
should also remember to simply wash and dry
it inside out. Reach inside the inside-out
cover – as though you're going to pull it
over your head – and grasp the two corners
of the opposite end. Still clutching the
cover, through the fabric, grab the two
end corners of the duvet. Flick the cover
over the duvet and lifting your hands as
high as possible – stand on the bed if you
like – shake like mad until the cover falls
down to the bottom of the duvet. Clip the
buttons or toggles at the bottom, shake out
at either end, and lay over the bed. Goodnight,
Goldilocks.

How to beat BO

Returning to the gym's changing room to discover a man in a radioactive suit brandishing a pair of your glowing Y-fronts and T-shirt is not a joyous experience, even if your favourite TV show is Doctor Who. *Like all your enemies, you have to know what makes BO tick to defeat it.*

Body odour comes from friendly bacteria munching on sweat and natural body oils. The bacteria has to stay because it's reducing the chances of infections taking hold all over our bodies, but we do want to limit the amount of lunch it has. In other words we want to limit what's on the menu. So, from head to toe, this is what you do to reduce the amount of sweat and oil we produce and keep bad odours at bay.

Head. Wash your hair at the roots at least every other day and more frequently when Mr Sun's out as this will remove dead skin and grease.

Bad Breath. Test your breath by licking the back of your hand and smelling the result, as this is far more effective than breathing into a cupped hand. Brush your teeth and your tongue at least twice a day, floss and drink lots of water as saliva trumps bacteria. Chewing on parsley can also sweeten bad breath, pineapple cleans the mouth with a friendly enzyme and a spoonful or two of unsweetened natural yoghurt will also reduce the bacteria. See your dentist for a check-up and visit the hygienist every six months.

Armpits. Deodorant will downplay odour, antiperspirants jam up your sweat glands and cotton clothes will absorb moisture and reduce sweat. If you're ever caught short with no deodorant, a good trick is to nab some bicarbonate of soda from the kitchen – pat it under your arms just like talcum powder to combat the pong. A splash of cider vinegar also does the trick. Don't wear the same shirt two days running. If you can't afford to buy a new wardrobe, wash your clothes on a hot cycle and this will help get rid of the smell better than washing on an eco-friendly cycle at 30°C.

Feet. Wash them daily, all over, and between the toes. If the problem persists, and you have unusually malodorous feet, try soaking your feet in a bowl of warm water with a couple of tablespoons of white vinegar. Do this for 10 to 15 minutes each morning before leaving the house. Dry feet thoroughly, and air them by wearing sandals and cotton socks; you never know, they might look nice with your Y-fronts and T-shirt.

How to survive sleeping rough for a night

For some people bus stops and bushes are more than just high-street furniture, they're a makeshift bed. Sleeping with only the twinkling of the stars for company is thought to be endured by up to as many as 75,000 young people every night in Britain, and if you're careless with your house keys, fall foul of your backdoor latch or miss the last train home you'll be living in their street under their rules.

Think of safety first. Find somewhere sheltered from the wind and rain; preferably somewhere you won't be spotted but not too far from civilization. Don't trust anyone you don't know and keep any items you own in your pockets.

Keeping warm is the next most important thing, so avoid sleeping directly on the ground with a hub cap for a pillow and bed down with some cardboard or newspapers. There are usually lots of unwanted newspapers in bins and cardboard outside shops. Try to cover your hands, feet and head as body heat escapes from these places first. Take a newspaper and wrap it round your midriff and back, against your skin, then pull your top down over it. Newspaper is extremely insulating and will help you retain body heat.

Snow is also a superb insulator if you happen to live in Alaska or get caught out at night in the Cairngorms – it takes five minutes to build a snow hole and is a lifesaver.

Once morning breaks, you'll return home covered in grime and dopey-eyed but the next time you pass someone on the streets you'll be able to empathize with their plight and flip them a thought, or even a coin.

How to impress your girlfriend's parents

'Deceased, the day he met my parents.' So reads the epitaph to many a relationship's tombstone. Here's a way to put a stop to one of love's most common killers.

Preparation. Do some revision about her parents' interests and lives so you can tailor your conversation winningly when you meet them. That way they'll see you as an intelligent, lively person, not just some lowlife Lothario desperate to get into their daughter's knickers.

First Impressions. **Dress smart. We're not talking cravat and braces, but shirt and jeans is a good start.**

The Greeting. A warm smile and a kind 'Nice to meet you' will suffice for Mum, but only a strong handshake will do for Dad. He's going to try to break your hand, so you better be ready and give as good as you get in return.

General Rules. Don't swear; address them as Mr and Mrs, not Mum and Dad (unless they tell you otherwise), don't make sexual comments to the daughter or the mother – it has happened. Be polite, but speak your mind, smile a lot and don't, whatever happens, lose confidence. Also, remember to butter them up and tell them what a witty, intelligent and lovely daughter they have. But don't overdo it; you don't want to give the impression you'd go on a killing spree if she dumped you the following evening. Don't be afraid to show your belle a bit of affection, but a full-on snog while Dad is saying grace is beyond the pale.

Table Manners. Compliment the cooking with enthusiasm and accept a plate of seconds no matter how unspeakable it is. Don't drink too much alcohol – throwing up in their toilet and urinating in the cat's litter tray won't win any Brownie (or Scout) points.

The Departure. If it looks like Mum wants a hug, don't disappoint. Doing the same to Dad might be overstepping the mark. If either want a kiss, keep your tongue in your mouth.

How to get a spider out of the bath without having a panic attack

---

Arachnophobia: the fear of spiders and a 1990s B-movie staring John Goodman and a papier-mâché tarantula a tripped-out Damien Hirst couldn't even cook up. Spiders are one of the few creatures that make grown men turn into little girls. Here's how to deal with the blighters.

If time is on your side, simply avoid all contact. Tear off a lengthy piece of toilet paper and drape it over the edge of the bath to create a makeshift ladder. Leave the bathroom and the next time you enter he'll have done a runner.

If immediate action is required – your lady wants a bath, *now* – grab a jam jar or mug and place it over the spider. He'll start scuttling around, so quickly slide a piece of hard cardboard under your receptacle and flick it upright, trapping the spider inside. Trek out to the garden, find a patch of grass, remove the cardboard lid, invert the jar and tap the lid until the spider topples out bleary-eyed and befuddled. When you return to the house, it is of paramount importance that you throw the contents of the empty jar over your girlfriend, who will respond by searching for the phantom spider down her top for the rest of the night. Either that or she'll dump you. If you're just going to fling the poor soul out of the nearest window, flick the jam jar several times until he's gone.

Feel like being a knight in shining armour? Use your hands. Cup them like you're drinking from a stream, leaving a gap at the fingers. Move towards the spider and surround him. Once he's in your finger cage close the gap. This will make him panic and leap about so resist the temptation to fling him into the corner and run from the room like you've just walked in on your mum in the shower, but keep your hands closed until you're outside.

Dispatching cobwebs is also easy. Bend a clothes hanger over into a smaller triangle and scoop the whole web up. Carefully place it outside in the bushes and you have reclaimed your home, masculinity intact.

Contrary to household myths, spiders don't come out of the plughole.
The U-bend, which is designed to stop things bunging up the drain and
halt the foul stench of the sewers, contains a couple of inches of water.
So unless the spider is a keen scuba diver he's not coming through. Where
they do come from is anyone's guess. What we do know is that they never
knock at the front door.

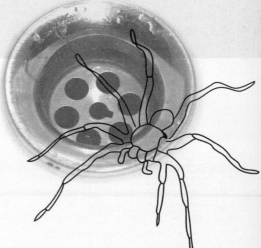

Spa etiquette

Latvians and Estonians beat one another with wet birch branches. Finns cool themselves down by running outside, diving into the snow and rolling about – all completely starkers. Germans and Austrians demand all visitors strip. While we, the brazen Brits, fall over ourselves apologizing if our private parts accidentally go public.

Follow these guidelines and make sure you don't pull a spa faux pas:

* Switch your phone off and talk like you're in a library or you'll be greeted with copious amounts of annoyed people putting their fingers to the lips and saying 'Shuuuuuush.'

* Use the robes and towels provided; tying a makeshift toga made of shower curtain around your waist isn't recommended.

* If you're in Latvia, there's no need to tear down a birch tree on your way. All thrashing equipment will be provided.

* Wear flip-flops. You might be sharing a sauna with an athlete, but you don't want to go home with his or her foot.

* Don't eat a heavy meal before entering the spa and don't take your egg mayo sandwiches in with you either. If you need to eat while you are there, stick to a healthy and inoffensive fruit salad or yoghurt.

* If you're booked in for a facial, have a shave two hours prior to the treatment.

* If you're worried about getting naked – don't. It's perfectly acceptable to wear swimming trunks. Greying old Y-fronts are less welcome.

* Use all the amenities on offer; if you've spent a lot of money, take your time and make the most of it.

Massage Tips:

* Take a warm shower before the massage.

* Drink plenty of water before and after.

* You can request to keep your underpants or swimmers on if you'd rather not go commando.

* Never drink alcohol before a massage – however, a massage is just the thing if you have a hangover.

* If you want a male masseur – God knows why – feel free to ask.

* If the new-agey music is too loud, the lights too low, or the temperature too hot – speak up.

* Likewise, if you prefer a stronger touch – if she's being too rough, inform her you're enjoying it.

* Take your time to leave the treatment room after the massage – but don't snuggle up and start to snore.

* You are not expected to talk – you're having a massage, not taking a taxi.

* It's quite common to get an erection mid-massage and very uncouth to do anything with it. Say no more.

Steam room and sauna rules:

* Don't wear swimming shorts with bits of metal on them or you'll be hopping like Tigger when they get hot and burn your bits.

* Remove glasses or contact lenses before a steam or sauna.

* Sit on your towel.

* Roughly fifteen minutes is about right for a sauna, six minutes for steam.

* Have a cold shower or a dip in the plunge pool between sessions to get the circulation going and cool you down.

* If you begin to feel dizzy or out of sorts leave straight away.

* The higher up you sit the hotter it will be in the sauna or steam room.

* Drink plenty of water.

Quick guide to shaving brushes

Invest in a badger-hair brush, not a cheap imitation. Badger hair is used due to its natural strength, enduring qualities, its ability to retain water and its overall softness. Note: no badgers were harmed in the making of this tip.

A brush's quality and price depends on the size of the handle and the quality and density of the hair. The best brushes are hand-made and made from the hair from a badger's neck – the best hair for water retention on the planet. They can cost from £25 to £500, but if you apply the foam properly a cheaper end brush will work fine.

There are three types of brush:

Pure. Dark hair with a coarser feel. *Short to medium length.*
Best. Greyish tip with a softer touch. *Medium to long length.*
Super. Cream-white tip, super-soft touch. *Longest length.*

* Always store the brush upright on its handle; you will damage the bristles if you rest it on its side.

* Look after your brush properly and it will serve you well for three years at least.

Blagger's guide to golf scores

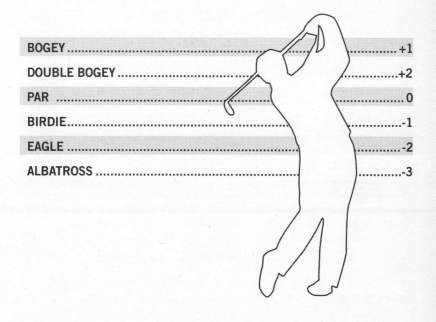

BOGEY	+1
DOUBLE BOGEY	+2
PAR	0
BIRDIE	-1
EAGLE	-2
ALBATROSS	-3

Blagger's quick imperial-to -metric conversion guide

INCHES TO CENTIMETRES .... *Multiply by 2.5*

YARD TO METRES .... *Subtract 10% (1m = 3.3 yards)*

MILES TO KILOMETRES .... *Multiply by 1.6 (or 8/5)*

FAHRENHEIT TO CELSIUS .... *Multiply by 5 and divide by 9 (roughly, take away 30, divide by 2)*

PINTS TO LITRES .... *Halve (1l = 1¾ pints)*

GALLONS TO LITRES .... *Multiply by 4.5*

POUNDS TO KILOS .... *Halve (1kg = 2¼lb)*

How to change a tyre like an AA man

Underworld. Netherworld. Inferno. Abode of the Damned. Hell has many names yet one true definition: finding yourself stranded on a country lane that looks like the film set of Deliverance *with a shrieking girlfriend, pouring rain, no battery on your mobile phone, a punctured tyre and no idea how to change it.*

Here's how to deal with the situation like a seasoned AA man.

Be prepared. As a driver it's up to you to make sure that your car is properly equipped for emergency breakdowns.

IN YOUR GLOVE COMPARTMENT, YOU SHOULD HAVE:

- *Vehicle handbook* which you should have read thoroughly and be able to recite on demand

- *Torch and spare batteries*

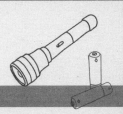

IN YOUR BOOT:

- *Hazard triangle*

- *Spare tyre* with adequate tread. If, like most men, you have never looked at your spare tyre, check it. In the worst-case scenario it could be one of those weedy 'trainer' wheels that looks more at home on a child's pedal car. And unless you drive a child's pedal car, it's not really going to help you out in a crisis.

- *A jack* suitable for your type of car

Tip: If you are nervous about changing a tyre, it might be a good idea to have a trial run at home in good weather and in daylight. Then you'll be more confident when you have to do it in an emergency situation.

- *Wheel-nut wrench* or *brace*
- *Wheel chock*

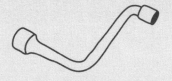

- *Something to kneel on* – not your girlfriend's coat, or her dog

- *Gloves*

- *Reflective jacket* for safety

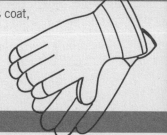

WHAT TO DO:

1. When you get a puncture, slow down and drive at no more than 5mph until you are at a lay-by or a side turning with a hard, smooth, level surface. Pull on the handbrake and put the car into either first gear (if pointing up a hill) or reverse (if pointing down one). If it's an auto, select 'park'.

2. Turn off the engine and turn on your hazard lights.

3. Get all passengers out of the car, for their safety. Yes, your girlfriend can suffer in the freezing cold with you. All passengers should move away from the car and well out of the road.

4. Place the hazard triangle at the side of the road to alert other drivers.

5. Chock the wheel diagonally opposite the flat tyre – a piece of wood or a brick will do.

6. Take out the spare tyre, the jack and the wheel brace from the boot.

7. Now remove the wheel cover with the end of the jack handle.

8. Next, position the jack as indicated in your owner's handbook – this is important as the jack will pierce the car's underside if it isn't placed beneath a strengthened area.

9. Then, without having jacked up the car and using the wheel brace, loosen the nuts on the wheel you intend to change by half a turn, but do not remove them. Turn counter-clockwise to loosen and try to loosen all the nuts equally.

10. Start pumping the jack; keep going until the flat tyre lifts off the ground by about 2–3 inches. Once the car body is raised sufficiently, push the spare wheel under the body; this will act as a safety cushion should the car slip off the jack. Unscrew the nuts in diagonal pairs, remove and place together in the upturned hubcap.

11. After having taken out the nuts, remove the wheel with your weight forward to stop you from falling backward. Fit the spare, ensuring it is the correct way round.

12. Fit wheel nuts in diagonal pairs and turn until finger-tight, but don't tighten them all the way.

13. Using the jack, lower the car until the tyre just kisses the road. Then, using the wheel brace, lightly tighten the wheel nuts.

14. Remove the punctured wheel from under the car, finish lowering the vehicle and remove the jack.

15. Finally, fully tighten the wheel nuts and get back on the road from hell. Don't forget to get the damaged tyre replaced or repaired as soon as possible – you never know when there'll be a next time.

How to tie the perfect full Windsor knot

For some modern males, the rule of thumb is the bigger the knot, the bigger the impact. Step up, the Windsor knot. This wide and triangular knot, the fat man of the tie world, is worn by most respectable men. And footballers.

Stand in front of the mirror; this makes sure you get all the crossovers correct and reduces the risk of auto-strangulation.

Lift up your shirt collar and place the tie around your neck.

Step 1. The fat end, **F**, should hang about twice the distance, 30cm or so, below the thinner end, **T**.

Step 2. Cross **F over T** and then bring **F up through the gap** between the collar of your shirt and tie as close to your neck as you can go without fainting. You've got to do this three times so don't allow the knot to get fat from the off.

Step 3. Pull **F back down, underneath T** and to the right and back through the loop to your right. By this point **F** will be inside out and the knot around your neck will be fairly fat.

Step 4. Bring **F across the front to the left**, pull it up through the loop and then, using a finger to widen the gap, push back down through the outer part of the loop you just made.

Step 5. Finally, tighten the knot carefully, adjust and straighten out. It should be tight to your neck, just below your Adam's apple, and there should be what's called a 'Vicious V' where the tie leaves the knot.

The fat part of the tie should hang about an inch above your belt buckle – two shirt buttons up from your waist – so if the thinner end hangs below try again with the fat end hanging lower down.

Step 1

Step 2

Step 3

Step 4

Step 5

In a professional setting, ties say a lot about our character so resist the temptation to take a school compass to it, just take your time and you'll get it right.

How to wolf whistle

Impress the foreman, stagger the lead singer and hail that cabbie with this blow-by-blow guide to the wolf whistle.

Stand in front of the mirror while you practise.

1. Pull your lips back, so that they are tightly pulled in over your teeth. You should now resemble a gummy old man. The outer edges of your lips might still be visible – this is fine.

2. Put your fingers in your mouth to pull your lower lip taut over your teeth. The fingers you choose depend on whether you have fat or thin fingers; a big or tiny mouth.

The choices are as follows:

* *U-shape with thumb and middle finger or index finger of one hand*

* *Right-hand and left-hand index fingers*

* *Right-hand and left-hand middle fingers*

* *Right-hand and left-hand little fingers*

3. Place each finger halfway between the corners and centre of your lips, to the first knuckle. Angle your fingernails inwards, towards the centre of your tongue.

4. Draw your tongue back so the tip touches the bottom of your mouth at the lower gums. Broaden and flatten it over your lower back teeth.

5. Inhale deeply and then exhale quickly, forcing your breath out over the top of your tongue and your lower lip. Experiment with your tongue position, the lips and finger positioning and the power of your blow, until you can hear a resemblance of a whistle. Blow gently at first and adjust until the pitch increases.

6. Once you have a weak-sounding whistle, you can perfect your technique to hone it to a strong, high-pitched and clear sound – which might come in handy if your parents' collie is running towards the M25. To do this you need to form a 'bevel'. This is an angled edge that, when air flows through it, creates a strong tone. You've found the 'sweet spot' when air is blown directly over the sharpest part of the bevel, maximizing the volume and tone of your whistle. You'll find the bevel and sweet spot by trial and error, varying your fingers and lip position.

7. Practise in front of a mirror when the mood takes you – it might take a week or two, but don't despair. When you hear that ear-piercing clear high-pitch you're on the money and an official member of the builders' union.

How to carve a chicken
like your dad

Sunday. You've had a lie-in, taken a bath, and read the papers. Songs of Praise *is on and the smell of a roast fills the house. Soon it will be time to carve the chicken. Here's how to show your dad how it's done.*

Remove the chicken from the oven, loosely cover with foil and leave to rest for fifteen minutes. This makes it easier to carve.

Lift the bird onto a chopping board and remove any string.

Use a very sharp carving knife and a fork to steady the bird.

Slide the knife down through the skin, between the body and the leg. Pull the thigh meat away from the bird, by wiggling the knife, until the joint is exposed. Chop down through the ball and socket joint to remove the drumstick and thigh. Divide the drumstick and thigh cutting at the joint. Remove the wings with a knife or by twisting them away by hand.

Push the knife carefully down one side of the breastbone and cut the whole breast away from the carcass. Slice the breast into portions.

Spin the chicken round and repeat on the other side.

Drop any scraps of meat to the baying crowd of cats, dogs and grandparents.

Present all the chicken pieces along with any stuffing or trimmings on a serving dish and watch as the family or guests devour it without any acknowledgement of your artistry.

Sports injuries breakdown

Like David Beckham in the 2002 World Cup and Wayne Rooney in the 2004 Euros, many a man's summer has been ruined by the dreaded metatarsal. The footballer's Achilles' heel, this seemingly insignificant little bone in the foot has plagued football fans and players for thousands of years.

Here's a list of other sporting ailments to be on the lookout for and how to treat them.

Runner's knee.

Symptoms. A swelling at the back of your knee and a grating sensation as you walk. Caused by running on hard surfaces such as pavements and roads.

Healing. Apply the PRICE regime and when you return to running stick to grass surfaces.

Tennis elbow.

Symptoms. Swelling on the outer edge of the elbow caused by an inflamed tendon. Your elbow will be tender to the touch and painful during movement, particularly pouring, gripping, lifting and opening doors. Can remain painful for up to 12 weeks.

Healing. Limit movement of your elbow for 2–3 weeks – so you'll have to use the other hand if indulging in self-pleasure.
Anti-inflammatory tablets, an elbow support or, if you're gearing up for the Wimbledon semi-final, a cortisone injection are also options.

Golfer's elbow.

Symptoms. As for tennis elbow, but affects the underside of the elbow.

Healing. The PRICE regime, limit movement, anti-inflammatory tablets and avoid the driving range for a few weeks.

Jogger's nipple.

Symptoms. Itchy and inflamed nipples caused by excessive chaffing during running, especially in wintery climes.

Healing. Liberally apply petroleum jelly before your brisk jaunt round the park to relieve pain and, in future, as a preventative measure.

Pulled muscles and strains.

Symptoms. Pulled and strained muscles cause pain, muscle spasms, loss of strength and possibly swelling.

Healing. Stick to PRICE regime, try a hot soak with Epsom Salts and for minor sprains and muscle strain apply Tiger Balm.

PRICE *is a healing regime used mostly for sprains and strains, however the principles apply for pretty much any sports injury:*

P – Protect the area with support such as a sling, if necessary.

R – Rest for at least 48–72 hours.

I – Ice. Use an icepack or a bag of frozen peas on the affected area for 10 minutes every 2 hours.

C – Compress the injury with bandages to reduce movement and swelling.

E – Elevate the body part on a pillow and get your mum to bring you tea.

How to overtake *like* Lewis Hamilton

When you're in a rush all the traffic lights turn red. Roadworks pop up out of nowhere. Normally bare zebra crossings become teeming with annoying people sauntering to the other side. And to cap it all you get stuck behind someone doing their best impression of Morgan Freeman in Driving Miss Daisy.

Here's how to overtake so Morgan won't see you for dust:

1. Even Galileo, Isambard Kingdom Brunel and Judith Chalmers rolled into one couldn't judge the speed of oncoming traffic. If in doubt pull back in.

2. Always indicate well in advance when waiting to overtake.

3. If you want to overtake more than one vehicle make sure the road is well clear ahead and that there is a sizeable gap between each car should you need to pull in sharply.

4. If you're tired do not overtake. You might be desperate for bed but a hospital bed shouldn't be considered an option.

5. Ask yourself at least three times if it's really essential to overtake the car in front.

6. When overtaking at night look for signs of oncoming headlights in the distance or round corners.

7. Give yourself extra distance when overtaking a lorry, both when behind and alongside.

8. Never overtake on corners, the brow of a hill, a bendy, windy road or before a humpback bridge. If the road ahead isn't straight don't even think about it.

9. Never attempt to overtake when there are turnings ahead as a car may pop up from nowhere.

10. After overtaking, pull in at a safe distance (at least a car length) and indicate back in.

How to tell if your pint of real ale is dodgy

Underage drinking followed a strict regime. Shuffle into the pub in a huddle. Brave the bar with hands wrist-deep in pockets. Snigger at the Bishop's Finger sign hanging over the bar. Order in the most inarticulate, inexpressive manner possible attempting to lower your voice so that any dogs in the vicinity don't start running for you. Cry at the sound of four half-pint glasses being filled with ice and Diet Coke.

But times move on and the true man will soon enough need to know how to spot a dodgy brew and when to return it. You wouldn't want to reject a perfectly poured pint, would you?

What to look out for:

Pipe cleaner still in pipes. A distinct taste of bleach should make the landlord take note and offer a fresh pint. A watery pint may well mean the pipes have been cleaned but the old beer hasn't been flushed through properly.

Premature pouring. A cloudy pint, sulphurous smell and metallic taste indicate inadequate resting time. Barrels of ale should be left to rest – 'laid to clear' in brewery speak – for at least a day.

Bacteria or yeast infection. A smell of sweat or sewage means the pub's pipes have a yeast infection. Or your mate needs a bath. Hazy beer is another indicator. If everything looks hazy, the beer's fine and it's you with the problem.

Dirty pipes. If your beer isn't as clear and shiny as a Crufts winner's coat, look for little globules floating about in the liquid – reminiscent of the spaceship in *Inner Space*, without Dennis Quaid of course.
Dip your finger into the head. If you pull it out and no amount of head sticks, you might be the victim of dirty pipes.

Keg laid too long. Old barrels produce beer with an insipid and flat taste. A lingering TCP tang, or vinegar flavour also indicate your beer is off.

Sunlight damage. The smell of cabbage or rotten eggs means the kegs have been left in the sunlight and earned more that a good tan.

Watered down. A watery taste may be caused by a lack of carbonization, an over-chilled glass as the icy condensation has 'watered' down the beer. Don't hesitate to ask for another.

Oxidization. Look out for how the barman pulls your pint. Smooth plunging motions ensure the beer isn't filled with oxygen. If the barman rushed the pouring and you end up with a beer smelling of wet paper, feel free to return it.

Problem with the glass. If the glass is too warm your beer will lose flavour. If the head is non-existent or quickly fading, the glass may be dirty.

Advanced tips:

Always compare your pint with one of your mates' before complaining.

Let the beer rest at room temperature before judging its cloudiness. A 'chilled haze' forms when the beer is still cold and won't dissipate until it warms up.

Real ales and lagers range from pitch black to light blonde, so know what your beer should look like before complaining.

Wheat beer will often be cloudy.

Be guaranteed a fresher pint by asking for popular ale – active lines mean a better pint.

Hop beer smells fruity and flowery. Malt beer will smell nutty with hints of caramel.

Some beers do have a strong yeasty aftertaste. Don't confuse a fault with your taste buds with a fault with the pub.

A good lasting head equals a good beer. No oral sex jokes please.

No matter how desperate you are, never drink out-of-date beer in cans or bottles.

How to give a massage *like a trained masseur*

Portuguese personal trainers called Antonio. Antiquarian bookdealers named Ray. Skinny tight-jeaned plumbers called Paul. Cuckolders come in many shapes and sizes. And none are more feared by men and revered by women than the trained masseur. Strolling into the room with a torso like a porcelain sculpture, swept-back black hair and a family heirloom hidden in his underpants. There's only one way to outdo the mighty masseur: become one yourself.

Setting the scene is your first task. Cracking open a can of Carling and mounting your girlfriend like she's Red Rum is not conducive to romance. Preparing a roaring log fire, lighting a few scented candles, placing a blanket on the floor and putting on her favourite mellow or soft music is.

A few pointers first:

* The room must be comfortably warm – warm enough to be naked. Massage brings the blood to the surface of the skin and can cool the recipient.

* A part of your skin should always be touching hers.

* Never ever apply pressure directly onto the spine or neck, you are not a chiropractor and will break her back.

* Use scented massage oil but don't grease up like a mechanic – you're rubbing someone's back not removing an engine. Different scented oils have different effects – lavender is relaxing, ylang ylang and rose are sensuous.

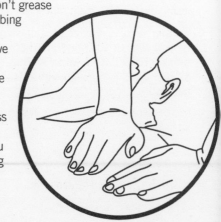

* Close your eyes and relax – unless you suddenly smell burning, in which case you'd better hope you don't open them to a reimagining of *The Towering Inferno* starring you, your girlfriend and a rather guilty-looking scented candle.

Fig. 1. Fan stroke

Fig. 2. Kneading

Once the mood is set you can begin:

Fan stroke. Relaxes and warms the muscles. Place your hands just above her hips and either side of her spine, with your palms down and fingers facing towards her neck. Gradually move them up to her shoulders, fan out to the ends and draw them back down along her ribcage, essentially making the shape of a falling teardrop. Do this eight or so times applying more pressure with each stroke.

Kneading. Get the blood flowing. Grip the flesh around her shoulders lightly between your fingers and the heel of your hands and working slowly and rhythmically squeeze the triangular muscle, the trapezius, beneath the skin. If she cries out you're probably pinching her and not, as your testicles are telling your brain, the genetically engineered lovechild of Daniel Craig and Russell Brand.

Milking. Deep muscle massage. Knead the muscle with one hand, remove it after one or two squeezes and replace with your other hand. Doing this milking relay will probably result in discovering hard 'knots' deep down in the muscle. Work these out using your palm and thumb. They'll keep moving about so give chase; ridding your lover of these little critters is where her back really benefits even if your hands don't.

Raking. Increases circulation. Place your fingertips on her shoulders and slowly rake all the way down to the bottom remembering to apply less and less pressure with each movement.

Feather touches. Rounds the massage off sensually. Repeat the raking motion without any pressure whatsoever. After a few downward strokes break off and doodle with your fingertips, draw invisible love hearts or play a solitary game of noughts and crosses until her groans cease and your hands tire.

Finally, kiss her on the neck and remove your hands at the same time. With any luck, and if she hasn't slipped a disc, her trapezius might not be the only muscle to get a squeeze tonight. Although if she hasn't moved after ten minutes expect nothing more than a lawsuit.

How to pull the perfect sickie

TODAY

Forget all those kung fu movies you've seen where the master has a long wispy beard and a balding head. The true master of speed and deception wears a suit and tie. Gentlemen, behold the art of the sickie-puller.

Timing your sickie or 'duvet day' is crucial, as is planning. The day before you plan to pull one, go into work a lot quieter than usual. As the day drags towards lunch begin to act out your chosen illness. Cough, wince when you swallow or visit the toilet every hour, but don't overdo it; spending the whole afternoon in the loo will arouse the wrong kind of suspicion. At the end of the day your colleagues will notice you're 'not yourself' and ask how you are. A simple, 'I don't feel great if I'm honest' will do and when you leave be sure to say, 'See you tomorrow' before you go.

The next morning make the phone call to work. Talk directly to your manager and sound like you're ill. Go into detail: 'It's coming out both ends and it just won't stop' will do the trick, but make sure it matches the illness you feigned the previous day.

For a really effective and more advanced sickie, take two days off. The phone call to your manager on the second day will be slightly different, but no less convincing, e.g. 'I'm still not quite right – I think I should take one more day at home but I'll be all right tomorrow I'm sure.'

Offer to have your work sent to you via email. The manager will decline, but he'll think you're a dedicated member of the workforce and not, as is the truth, a lowly skiver. You can spend the rest of the day doing whatever you like. Just don't go anywhere near your place of work; that's pull-a-sickie-suicide.

The next day act like you did the day you set the sickie up just switch it round. Act ill in the morning and then by the end of the day leave with a spring in your step and a smile on your face.

January 2nd is traditionally the most popular day of all to pull a sickie – according to one survey it's estimated that on that day in the UK five million workers call in sick, and over a year sickies are thought to cost the UK economy up to £4billion.

How to clean your bathroom, toilet and shower
in a quarter of an hour

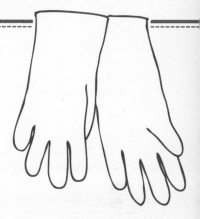

Everyone likes a bath, no one likes cleaning one. But it's a job that must be done, so just do it quickly.

Marigolds. The connoisseur's choice and the bathroom cleaners' first line of defence against the evil forces of the porcelain bus. They should be slapped against the wall like an earl's glove to the face of his duelling nemesis.
Pulled on like the king's jewel-encrusted gauntlets. Cherished until the war is won and then discarded, removed inside out like a disembowelled Sooty, and never ever used to do the washing-up. The rules of the Marigold are a simple affair and so too are the steps to achieving a showroom bathroom in fifteen minutes.

Step 1. **Assemble your tools.** You need some powerful toilet cleaner with a bent nozzle, toilet brush, sponge or cleaning rag, a roll of toilet paper, bathroom spray, shower cleaner cream and a shammy.

Step 2. **Sink.** Clear away toothbrushes, razors, soap, etc. and wipe the sink clean with toilet paper. Spray the basin, tiles and mirror with the bathroom cleaner, leave for a minute or two and wipe clean with the shammy. Run hot water and wipe once more until glistening pristinely.

Step 3. **Toilet.** Don the Marigolds. Squeeze the toilet cleaner around the bowl making sure the nozzle is right up under the rim. The colourful liquid should ooze down into the water like a psychedelic Niagara Falls. Grab the toilet brush and shove it in there too. Scrub vigorously with the toilet brush all around the bowl removing any unsightly stains and clinging matter. Lift the toilet seat and use the cleaning rag to wipe all around the toilet rim and clean the underside of the seat too. Rinse your cloth thoroughly between wipes. Last, lower the seat and wipe it clean. Flush to rinse, making sure the toilet brush gets a good rinse too. Add a dash of bleach or white vinegar to the toilet bowl to sanitize, whiten and add a suitably disinfected smell to your lavvy.

Step 4. **Shower.** Get naked bar the Marigolds, make sure the blinds are drawn – unless you're into that kind of thing – and get in with the cream and shammy. Squirt cream all over the walls of the shower, if it's a walk-in, or all over the bath, if it's a bath, and wipe it all around. Leave for a couple of minutes. Fold your shammy over and vigorously wipe around the shower, including head, dials, taps, etc. until all the cream is removed. Use a wad of toilet roll to fish out any hair and pubes from the plughole. Put in the bin or in the toilet and flush.

Step 5. **You.** Remove the gloves and throw them over the top along with the shammy and cream. Turn the shower on, clean your whole body twice with shower gel, grab a towel and step out victorious into your sparkling bathroom.

How to out-buff a film buff
when you know nothing about film

There's nothing more annoying than a film buff chatting up the same girl as you, impressing her with his knowledge of Ingmar Bergman's The Seventh Seal *or the complete works of Kurosawa. So rather than embarrassing yourself and quoting* Police Academy II *here's how to keep up with the conversation and win back her attention.*

The chances are the film buff will mention at least one of the following directors, and even if he doesn't you'll blow him away with these cinematic pearls of wisdom.

1. If the conversation strays towards the early days of film simply say: 'For me Welles [Orson] reinvented the way stories are told when he made *Citizen Kane* – and to think he was only 26. Unbelievable.' *Don't say, 'The colours are amazing.'*

2. If horror and suspense crops up try this one: 'For me there's no one like Hitchcock. *Vertigo* is out of this world. A detective story about darkness and desire starring James Stewart. Need I say more?' Don't try … lest you out yourself as a film dud.

3. As far as gangster movies go you can't go wrong with this: '*The Godfather.* Brando, Pacino, Keaton, Duvall, Caan. It really is a who's who of Hollywood.'

4. If none of the above fit the bill a mention of Stanley Kubrick or Woody Allen won't go amiss, but you'll often get asked to back up your namedropping by citing your favourite movie. For Kubrick it's got to be *2001: A Space Odyssey* but, beware, a true fan would just say '*2001*'. As for Allen, it's a toss-up between *Manhattan* and *Annie Hall*; both are romantic and give you the opportunity to say to the girl: 'The main character reminds me of you. She is witty and intelligent.'

Congratulations, you've out buffed a film buff without resorting to violence. And if you rush, you'll just make it home in time for Police Academy III.

How to wash your clothes
like your mum

*In your teenage years washing your smalls
was part of your mum's job description.
Once in your twenties or, heaven forbid,
your thirties, you're fast approaching
mummy boy status if your dear old ma is
still dealing with your Y-fronts.*

Go on. Be a real modern man, and learn how to do your own washing
without shrinkage or dying everything pale grey.

Laundry dos and don'ts:

* Divide your clothes into whites, darks and denims, and colours and
  wash separately.
* Wash towels separately to keep fluff off your designer T-shirts.
* If your towels or gym socks are smelly and musty, try adding a
  cupful of white vinegar to the fabric softener compartment.
* Colours that might run – it should warn you on the label –
  should be washed separately. Be extra wary of new denims and red
  clothes.
* Avoid high temperatures except for washing white towels and bed
  linen. If in doubt use 30° on a normal wash.
* Never put woollens in hot water – only wash in the machine if
  you have a 'Wool Wash' option, otherwise hand wash. Never
  hang woollens to dry – dry flat to prevent them losing shape
* Silk should only be dry-cleaned or carefully hand washed –
  remember that when your girlfriend leaves her incredibly expensive
  one-of-a-kind-knickers lying about the place.
* Don't overload the washing machine.
* Liquid or powder detergents should be poured into the dispenser.
  Tablet detergents placed in the net bags (supplied with your pack)
  at the back of the machine on top of your clothes.
* Fabric softener should be placed in a separate dispenser and only
  used if you like the feel of soft fabric on your skin, you big girl.

Guide to washing symbols

Hand wash only in warm water. Rinse and dry carefully.

Machine wash at the shown temperature in Celsius.

30° - Coloured delicates.

40° - Coloured T-shirts and pants.

60° - Very soiled clothes.

95° - White sheets and towels.

Lines underneath the machine wash symbol inform you of the type of programme you should use.

No line – Max speed/cotton programme.

One line – Moderate speed/synthetic programme.

Two lines – Minimal speed/wool programme.

OK to bleach.

No bleach.

No dot – No temperature restriction.

One dot – Maximum temperature of 60°.

Two dots – Normal dry.

Tumble dry at your own risk.

Hang dry.

Dry flat.

Ironing allowed.

One dot – Cold iron, 110° max. Acrylic, nylon and acetate.

Two dots – Hot iron, 150° max. Polyester and wool.

Three dots – Very hot iron, 200°. Cotton and linen.

Do not iron.

Dry clean only. The letter and lines indicate special dry cleaning instructions.

Do not dry clean.

There are sometimes other written instructions below the symbols.

Wash like colours together.

Reshape while damp.

Iron on reverse – i.e., iron inside out to preserve logos or printed colours.

Wash inside out.

Blagger's guide to cricket fielding positions

Sledging: a form of putting off the opposition during a game of cricket. The most famous sledge of all time came during an Aussie test match against the Zimbabweans. When the Australian fast bowler asked the African batsman why he was so fat, he simply replied, 'Because every time I f**k your wife she gives me a biscuit'.

On a tamer note here are all the options available to a cricket captain when he's setting out his field.

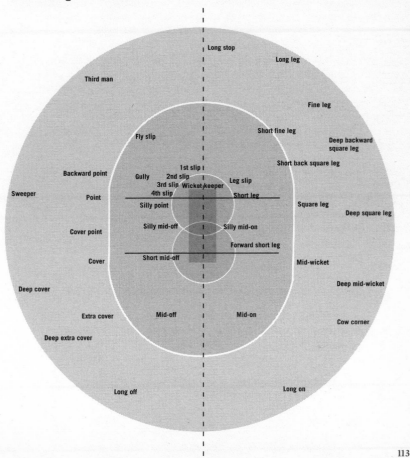

What flowers to buy for different occasions

Whether for your mother, sister or girlfriend, buying a woman flowers can be a minefield. Turn up to a birthday bash with a petrol station bouquet of frayed petals and flimsy stalks and you might find yourself wearing the bouquet down the back of your trousers.

Take on board this little lesson in the language of flowers, on the other hand, and you'll be heralded as a model gentleman:

To say sorry. It may be the hardest word, but so much easier to say with flowers. The rare blue rose symbolizes peace, and being hard to come by will earn you extra brownie points. Daisies are said to cheer people up and mark new beginnings. Hydrangeas represent understanding, tulips and hyacinths forgiveness, and bluebells suggest sorrowful regret. Alternatively, you could give her a guilt trip with a handful of withered flowers, the symbol of rejected love and petrol stations.

Anniversary or Valentine's Day. Forget-me-nots for true love, constancy and memories. Cacti, despite being prickly, symbolize endurance. Red roses are a little passé, but if you must go for them buy one or a dozen – eleven red and one white with the white representing your one true love. Just be prepared for the question, 'Who do the others represent, you cheating bastard?'

Mother's Day. Yellow flowers are bright and cheery and symbolize adoration, gracefulness and friendship. Dahlias, elegance and dignity, magnolias, magnificence and benevolence, and violets loyalty.

Grandma's birthday. Pink roses sit well with the oldies as they speak of friendship. Purple flowers are often related to royalty and admiration – perfect for the Queen Mum in your life. Irises denote faith and wisdom. A word of warning: don't send Granny orange flowers or chrysanthemums, or worse orange chrysanthemums (orange symbolizes lust! And, well, chrysanthemums are usually put on graves).

How to look after a beard

Whether you're going for David Beckham's sexy stubble or Giant Haystack's bear impression, a beard trimmer with various guard settings is a must-have.

1. Start on a high guard grade and use a range of settings over a few months to find the right look and grade for you.

2. When you trim, don't soak your beard as this could damage the trimmer. Only slightly wet it.

3. Use a normal razor, or unguarded trimmer, to shave on the underside of your chin.

4. Set the trimmer to your usual setting and clip the upper horizontal edges symmetrically.

5. Vertically run your trimmer along the jawline, from ear to chin, in one smooth and steady motion. This will ensure an even clipping. You should be left with a finger's thickness of hair on the underside of your jawline.

6. Run the trimmer over your cheeks, if needed several times, ensuring you are guided by your face's undulations and contours. Wash your beard to remove all clippings.

7. Random grey hairs can be banished with some tweezers – if you're brave.

8. Once you start to trim your beard it will get bushier so be prepared to wield the scythe every other day at least.

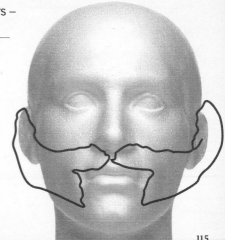

How to survive your first poker night

If you're not careful, the first night you play poker can turn into one long, prolonged wave goodbye to your week's wages. So read carefully because there are certain ways you can reduce the amount you lose, and possibly even take home someone else's salary.

1 *First of all.* Watch the other players. Note what hands they win with and what hands they fold on.

2 *Secondly.* Play a couple of hands yourself, but only bet small amounts of money. It sounds boring and reserved – and it is – but playing safe won't result in you having to choose between telling your dad his Lexus is now owned by Joey 'Four Fingers' Capone, or giving one of your own fingers to Joey.

3 *Thirdly.* Use your circumstances to your advantage. It's your first night at the table so people will call you when you bet, but eventually you'll be dealt a good hand. When this happens, play aggressively, and if you're certain you're on to a winner don't be afraid to bully the other players with big bets.

4 *Fourth.* Bluffing rarely works. If you want to give it a go, don't try to bluff more than one player at a time because you're more likely to get caught out.

5 *Last, but not least.* If you know someone's got a better hand just fold. It's the person with the most money, not the biggest ego, who goes home happy.

Facial grooming for grown-ups

One day you're staring up at your dad's chin covered in shaving cream, longing for the day when you too will have a whiskered chin of your own. The next, you're staring in the mirror at your sprouting nostrils wondering when the hell you morphed in to Chewbacca. Nobody wants to be that hairy.

Here's a step-by-step guide to taming your face and extraneous body hair:

Eyebrows

While you're still young, if you are lucky this will mainly be a case of plucking the odd unruly long and wiry ginger hair every now and then.

But if your brows verge on Denis Healey proportions, you might need more remedial treatment:

1. Plucking: pluck after a warm shower. This opens up the pores and makes it less painful. Use clean, slanted tweezers and pluck between the brows to eradicate the mono-brow. Tweezer a single hair at a time, grasp close to the root and pull, not yank, in the direction of growth.

2. If your eyebrow hair is unusually long, trim back with scissors.

3. Pluck out the odd stray hair above and below the eyebrow line, but don't overdo it – you don't want to end up looking like Boy George.

Waxing

Ideal if you sport the my-father-married-his-sister-and-I'm-the-result look. Done by a professional it will prolong the time your mono-brow is banished for. On the other hand, if you don't want to enter a salon and say, 'Will you wax my uni-brow today?' you can do it yourself in five minutes.

*   Use small wax strips specifically designed for facial hair.

*   Place the strip between your eyebrows.

*   Smooth over and, pulling your forehead taut, whip the strip off in an upward motion.

*   Wipe the waxed area with tea tree or aloe vera lotion to calm redness and prevent spots.

Ears and nostril hair

Hair trimmers work wonders and most cost under a fiver. And much less painful than tweezers! Always blow your nose first.

How to save money *as well as the environment*

Saving the world can save you money. Make your house an energy-efficient paradise without living in a box room lined with kitchen foil eating the flotsam and jetsam leftovers of the fast-food tide.

* Lower your central heating thermostat by just one degree and knock 10% off your total heating bill.

* Don't leave the TV, computer, stereo, etc. on stand-by.

* Unplug mobile phone and iPod chargers when they're not being used.

* Dry clothes on the line outside or fit an old-fashioned clothes airer to the ceiling. Tumble dryers should only be used on rare emergency occasions.

* **Energy efficient light bulbs** might take a while to heat up and leave you feeling like you're standing in a dungeon for fifteen minutes, but they do **save you about £9 a year and last about ten times longer**.

* Check that your roof is efficiently insulated.

* Take showers rather than a baths. An average bath uses 40 to 45 gallons of water, whereas taking a five-minute shower uses only about 15 to 20 gallons of water.

* PCs use more energy than laptops, so get a laptop.

* Get a high-efficiency, condensing boiler which could cut your heating bill by up to a third.

* Install a wind turbine, heat pump or wood-burning stove.

* Recycle everything you can and make regular trips to the local recycling bank.

* Use rechargeable batteries.

* Wash your clothes on a low-temperature 30°C wash and invest in Eco-balls rather than using traditional detergents.

* Grey water systems, whereby the water from your washing up and shower gets transferred to your toilet cistern, can also be installed. The world and your wallet might be the least of your worries however, if you get the pipes mixed up.

How to live on £40 a week
and still have a social life

How often do you find yourself scrabbling down the side of the sofa in the hope of finding a stray pound coin or two? And desperately searching in old coat pockets for the odd ten pence? Counting coppers isn't much fun for anyone. But sometimes needs must, so here's how to live on the breadline or the dole and still have a life.

Assuming rent, bills and council tax have already been paid, and you don't run a car, forty quid a week can go a long way.

Be strict. Every Sunday night go to a cash point and withdraw £40. This is a good way of keeping track of your money – if you haven't got any in your wallet you won't spend it. This should be the only time you visit the bank all week.

Next up, first thing Monday, it's the supermarket. Be careful what you buy. Meat is expensive so limit yourself to one portion of streaky bacon or sausages and make them last. Cutting down on meat will do wonders for your waistline, too. And vegetarians live longer, apparently.

Keep your store cupboard stocked up with durable items such as rice, tinned tomatoes or dried pasta. Baked beans and eggs are also good staples. **Always opt for the supermarket's own brand or 'basic buy' range.** Having base ingredients means you only have to buy fresh vegetables and the essentials such as milk, butter and bread. Also, bargain hunt and freeze any reduced pieces of meat for the following week.

Shopping like this will cost you between £10 and £20, leaving you up to £30 to play with.

Planning is the key to optimizing your pennies. If footie's on the box, buy **eight cans for a fiver,** and the cinema only costs about £6, leaving you about a tenner to buy a round with on Saturday night. That's three nights out of seven you'll be busy. Not bad for £40.

Alternatively, save the thirty quid for a big night on the town. Neck cans of cheap lager before you go out so you have enough to pay the extortionate prices in the pubs and clubs.

Two more tips to remember. Take your lunch to work and utilize all the free stuff in this country. Art galleries, libraries, books, TV and radio, let alone the internet, all provide free entertainment. Follow these rules and £40 can feel like £4,000…or £400 at least.

How to rewire a plug *without* burning your house down

In a world of moulded plugs, the modern man doesn't have to do this very often, but before you end up in A&E with a silhouette of a screwdriver burned into your hand, here's what to do if your old plugs need mending. Start by unscrewing the plug cover and check the colours of the wires. They are as follows:

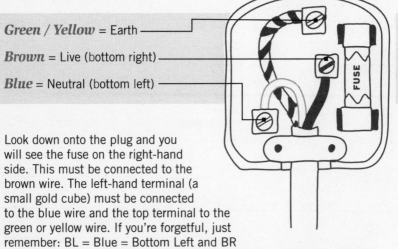

Green / Yellow = Earth

Brown = Live (bottom right)

Blue = Neutral (bottom left)

Look down onto the plug and you will see the fuse on the right-hand side. This must be connected to the brown wire. The left-hand terminal (a small gold cube) must be connected to the blue wire and the top terminal to the green or yellow wire. If you're forgetful, just remember: BL = Blue = Bottom Left and BR = Brown = Bottom Right. The earth wire is easily remembered because it is the longest pin. When pushed into the socket, it acts as a locking mechanism and releases the other two holes for the electrical current to pass through. Once located, connect the wires by unscrewing the screws with a screwdriver and pushing the wires underneath. Now screw the screw back in. Finally, screw the cable clamp in place at the bottom of the plug and screw the top back on.

How to prepare your CV for a job application

CV, or Curriculum Vitae, comes from the Latin, 'course of life'. This is the perfect way to remember what it is you're writing about. Your CV should be a record of your occupational and educational life but also give an impression of the general direction your life is taking. 'Course of life' incorporates previous achievements and future potential – bear this is mind when constructing your CV.

First impressions

*   Keep it simple – a heart-shaped 30-page embroidered felt booklet might stand out from the rest of the pack but it will also make the manager think you're an egomaniac from hell with a fetish for felt.

*   Keep it brief – two pages of A4 maximum, typed on clean and unfolded paper.

*   Use black ink, so it can be photocopied, in Arial or Times New Roman size 10 and 12 font, and number the pages.

*   Put your name at the top in larger font.

*   All headings in bold and sub-headings in italics.

*   Leave spaces between each heading. Anal? A little. Job-worthy? Certainly.

*   Use short paragraphs, bullet points and simple language. Not slang, innit?

Add your contact details to the bottom of each page – email, address, home and mobile number. If you live at home inform your parents you're expecting some calls about work. Don't forget to help your father off the floor.

* Use a sensible-sounding email address. Bigballs@aol.com or similar is perfect.

* If emailing your CV use Microsoft Word. This is the format nearly everyone on the planet uses and if prospective employers can't open your document they'll just move on to the next one.

* Photos – especially that one of you being violated by a blow-up sheep in Ibiza – should not be included.

* Personal details such as marital status, age and disabilities are not required unless you are requested to fill in an Equal Opportunities form.

* Double-check dates and spelling. Then double-check again. Bad grammar and spelling are not selling points.

Tailor the order of your CV to the position you are applying for. An entry-level job should detail education, then previous employment and interests and hobbies. For more experienced positions, lead with jobs, then education, with hobbies last. Use your initiative and give yourself the best chance to stand out. Putting your hobbies first will also make you stand out. As a lunatic.

Mission or personal statement

This is a paragraph declaring who you are, what you have to offer and where you see yourself in the next few years. Think about your experience and skills which are relevant to the job you're applying for.

Example: 'Qualified electrician with three years experience as an apprentice seeks corporate company offering large contracts throughout the British Isles.'

Occupation history

* Don't overplay your achievements and never lie on your CV.

* List your job history, from the present back. Include the month and year you started and finished, then the company name and job title e.g. January 1999 – August 2002 – Boddiswell House, Hotel Porter.

* Under each job title, list a summary of core skills. Prioritize according to the job you're applying for. Plumbing firms are probably not going to be interested in cake decorating skills. List all key skills, from most important, e.g. management, to more secondary, e.g. basic Quark training.

* Negotiating, presentation, touch-typing, cash handling, public speaking, stock ordering and rota organization are all skills – so list them where appropriate.

* Fill in any unemployment periods with some information, e.g. 'Went travelling around Africa' or 'Took a break from work to reassess my life.' Don't put 'Won "Championship Manager" twice in a row with Scunthorpe FC.'

* Reduce the amount of info for older and less relevant jobs. Temping jobs for example can be reduced down to 'Temping' with basic skills.

* Include unpaid or voluntary work. This gives an insight into your personality and perseverance.

* Anything that might be relevant is worth jotting down as long as you put it in its rightful place and keep it brief and informative. Working for a corporate company in your teens – such as McDonald's or Spar – shows you can pull your weight in an international organization.

* Read the job descriptions and pick out key words and attributes. If it says 'Looking for adaptable person' include the word 'adaptable' in your CV and back it up with proof from past roles.

Education history

* Follow the same format as your occupation history with achievements you gained in each institution.

* Include extra-curricular feats: rugby captain, contributor to student magazine, annual 'Guitar Hero' competition organizer, etc.

* Other courses such as food hygiene and first aid should also be included here.

Hobbies and other activities

* Use your hobbies to paint a three-dimensional picture of your life. Sports show you can work in a team, blogging shows a good understanding of modern media and running the local pub quiz can show good presentation skills.

* Be selective about which interests you disclose. Personalize your CV, by all means. But stay within acceptable limits. If you wouldn't tell a barman, you probably shouldn't include it here.

References

* Include a work reference and a character or academic one. Don't put down your Aunt Agnes, even if she does think you're a lovely boy.

* Include job titles, company name, company address, email and phone number of your referees.

Cover letter

* You should have an introductory paragraph much like the one at the start of your CV.

* Include a longer, middle paragraph expanding on the skills you've acquired from jobs, education and hobbies.

* The final paragraph should refer to your possible relationship with the company and state how and why you would be an ideal candidate for the job. Use 'I' freely here. For example, 'I consider myself a very competent person able to perform under pressure as my experience with the fire service shows.'

* If your career path has changed radically over the years, now is a good chance to explain why.

Where to put things in the fridge

The male mind short-circuits at the thought of housework of any kind. Vacuum cleaners make us weak at the knees. Feather dusters bring us to tears. But nowhere is this more evident than in the case of a man's fridge. Though he opens and closes its smelly door a hundred times a day, hoping that perchance some new tasty snack will have miraculously been beamed in from Tesco, a young male will remain blissfully oblivious to the gruesome sights and malevolent smells issuing from every festering cranny ... Until the day, perhaps, when a new girlfriend delves in, and has to undergo trauma counselling before coming round for toast ever again ...

Keep your fridge in order and keep your girlfriend out of therapy. Here's how.

* First, undertake a major overhaul of your fridge hygiene.

* Remove everything from the fridge. Be brutal and dispose of anything that looks unpleasant or is past its sell-by date.

* Put all the shelves and detachable vegetable drawers in the sink and fill with clean, warm water. Add detergent. Wash thoroughly. Add a cupful of white vinegar to the last rinse for extra squeaky cleanness and to remove bad odours. Allow to air-dry.

* Clean the inside of the fridge thoroughly using a clean cloth and a bowl of warm water. Again, add a splosh of white vinegar or lemon juice to the final rinse to kill any bacteria and remove odours.

* Once dry, replace all the shiny clean shelves and drawers.

Now start as you mean to go on:

Vegetable drawer. Make sure air can circulate around the drawer – don't keep it packed full or you risk your greens going limp. Preferably use two separate drawers – or divide your drawer in two. Keep fruits, salad and other leafy vegetables such as broccoli, spinach, celery and rocket in one as they lose moisture faster and will soak other veg. Use the other side for any other vegetables listed below (with a rough guide to how long they will keep the fridge).

Door shelf. Keep milk and fruit juice here, as well as ketchup, mayonnaise and mustards. An open bottle of champagne and white or rosé wine lasts about four days in the fridge; add a silver spoon to keep bubbly bubbly.

Bottom shelf. The coolest part of the fridge. Store raw meat and fish here, wrapped in their packaging straight from the shop. Keep all raw meats separate to avoid contamination, and never mix raw and cooked foods on same plate. Wrap raw meat in tin foil and place a plate under larger joints – such as a leg of lamb – as an extra precaution to keep the fridge clean. Blood running over your salad is probably a step too far for most.

Beer shelf. Lay beer cans on their sides carefully to rest and to maximize shelf space.

Cheese box. Pongy Stilton gets everywhere so seal it up with clingfilm, as tight as Tutankhamen's tomb.

Top shelf. This is the warmest part of the fridge, so remember, food which isn't in jars or wrappers might not last as long here. Store opened jars of jam, butter, and any left-overs to be eaten soon on this shelf.

Advanced tips:

* Don't let food touch the sides or back of the fridge as this can make it freeze.

* Don't store certain foods together. Apples turn carrots bitter because of the ethylene gas they give off. Potatoes should be kept in a paper bag on their own as they can rot onions. Store garlic on its own or everything else will smell like a vampire slayer's neck.

* A brown paper bag will stop vegetables becoming sweaty and wet. Vegetables or fruit kept in plastic packaging will last longer if taken out and stored loose in the fruit bowl or vegetable drawer in the

fridge. Don't keep fruit and veg in airtight containers.

* Line your vegetable drawer with paper towels to quicken the annual – if you can be arsed at all – clean.

* Never keep food in an opened tin as this can cause serious illness and several trips to the loo. Store the remaining contents in a covered bowl or your grandma's hand-me-down Tupperware.

* Anything bought from the chilled section of a shop should be kept in the fridge.

* Warm food should be allowed to cool before being put in the fridge. Cover with clingfilm and store in the fridge for up to two days.

* As a general rule, anything you can't remember putting in the fridge should be taken out and disposed of immediately.

* Baking soda gets rid of any odours hanging about; pour into a small glass or egg cup, and make sure you change the baking soda regularly to keep pongs at bay. As long as you don't take a short cut past the local sewage works.

* Check your manual and keep the fridge temperature at the optimal setting.

FOOD LIFE

O Mushrooms – 1–2 days

O Asparagus, berries, cherries – 2–3 days

O Plums, kiwis, French beans, peas – 3–5 days

O Melons, cauliflower, cabbage, green beans, chillies, peppers – 1 week

O Beetroots, radishes, carrots – 2 weeks

O Cranberries, lemons, limes and grapefruits – more than 2 weeks

O Apples – 1 month

O NB: eggs, potatoes, tomatoes, mangoes, avocados, bananas, garlic, onions, squash, lemons, oranges and apples do not need to be stored in the fridge.

Cut out and stick to front of fridge

Blagger's guide to knots

Tying up a boat, an abseiling rope or possibly even the girlfriend requires a steady hand and a keen eye. But if you don't know what knot to use or how to tie it, you could end up with a shattered starboard, a comatose climber or a bitter bride-to-be.

From light bondage to scouting skills, here's a blagger's guide to knots.

Boating knots:

Bowline:

This knot forms a secure loop making it ideal for mooring a boat to a pole or ring.

Allowing for the size of the knot, form a loop at the end of the rope. Slot the end of the rope through the loop, round the back of the main rope and down through the loop to finish.

Cleat Hitch:

Used for tying a rope to a dock cleat.

Pull the rope round the left-hand side of the cleat. Loop the rope round the horn – ohhh, matron – and cross over the cleat. Pass the rope under and over to form a figure of eight. Round the cleat once more and finally pull tight between rope and cleat.

Double Fisherman's knot:

Considered by many climbers to be the best knot to tie two ropes, or two rope ends, together.

Place the two ropes alongside and then over each other. Dealing with one rope first, pass its end under both ropes. Wrap the rope round twice. Pass through the ends and pull tight. Repeat the process with the other rope so you have two symmetric knots. Pull both ropes tight so the knots fit snug together.

Prusik knot:

A slide and grip knot, this knot tightens when pressure is applied and can be slid up or down when under no strain.

Get a piece of cord or rope tied together using a Fisherman's knot and pass it over another rope. Pull the Fisherman's rope back through the loop. Repeat this two more times until you're left with six loops around the rope. Pass the Fisherman's knot through the loop and pull tight to finish.

131

Palomar knot:

Strong and reliable, this knot is used to secure a fishing line to a hook.

Looping the end, push the rope through the eye of the hook. Pass the loop under the rope and through the second loop you've just formed. Pull the loop over the hook. Tighten the knot and snip the end off.

Arbor knot:

One of the most common knots used to attach the fishing line to the reel. Loop the line around the reel or arbor and back and under the line. Tie a standard or overhand knot. To prevent the first knot from slipping, tie a second overhand knot with the same end to finish.

Reef knot:

Used to join two equal length ropes together.

Cross two rope ends over. Pull the ends up – one under, one over. Tie the two loose ends together and pull tight.

Double Overhand Stopper knot:

Frequently used to secure a rope to stop it slipping through a pulley, another knot, etc.

Loop the rope round itself. Repeat. Slot the end of the rope through the turns and pull snug.

How to buy a suit *without getting ripped off*

There will come a time when one of your mates gets married, and when it comes you don't want to be the loser who turns up in Bermuda shorts and a Hawaiian shirt. You'll need to wear a suit. But before you go out and buy one there are a couple of things you need to do.

Firstly, set yourself a budget and, secondly, measure your collar, chest, waist and leg length. When you've done that, have a look in several shops and see what styles you like.

When it comes to trying on the suit, be wary of several things. The shoulders should hug yours; if you stand sideways against a wall your arms should touch the wall before the shoulder pads do. Also, you should be able to button up the suit without straining and there shouldn't be too much space between buttons and chest; about a fist's worth is a good guide. The trousers should rest on the top of your shoes and you should be able to put your hands in your pockets with ease.

Finally, lift your arms above your head. The suit shouldn't ride up at the back and the cuffs should meet the palm of your hand when you curl your fingers back.

One extra tip: Buy a spare pair of suit trousers; the jacket always outlives the trousers, and the last thing you want is to wear a jacket and jeans – unless you want to look like your 'trendy' dad.

1 Fabric – worsted wools wear well and are typically good year-round depending on where you live.

2 Your sleeve should just reach the base of your thumb, revealing a half-inch to an inch of your shirt cuff – very classy.

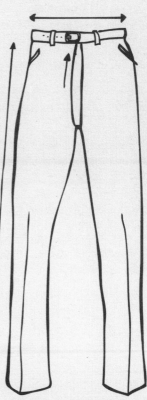

3 Make sure that the waistline of your trousers is comfortable and that you can stick two fingers into the waist while you're wearing them.

4 Your trouser should reach your shoes and have a slight break.

Note: Cuffless trousers make you look taller if you happen to be a little shorter and cuffs looks better on someone with long legs.

Love on a budget: cheap but romantic dates

2 for 1 deals

Crash an art gallery opening

Home cinema with popcorn

Or see, massage tips, p.104

There's nothing more romantic than holding hands with the woman you love, sunlight dancing in her hair, lips aquiver in the breeze, safe in the knowledge you haven't opened your wallet once. Here's how to tighten your belt on a date without reducing the chances of your lady unbuckling it later.

Head for a beach. Pack a romantic picnic for two. Cucumber sandwiches and a silver platter are probably a little over the top, but a miniature bottle of her favourite wine, a rug and a punnet of ripe strawberries and a selection of nibbles might result in a nibble of a different kind. Linger until sunset, then wrap her up in a shawl and take a moonlit stroll along the deserted beach.

Art gallery or museum. Impress her with your range of cultural knowledge spanning from Byzantine murals to Warhol's *Soup Cans*.

Go boating. Rent a boat for the day and watch her eyes twinkle with delight as you attempt to untangle yourself from your fishing line for the umpteenth time.

Night in the city. Wrap up and take a moonlit stroll along the lonely city streets at midnight. Romance will blossom in your isolation and before long you'll be discussing the names of your future children and picking out the curtains for your family home in the Cotswolds.

Late and great gift ideas for girlfriends

Your girlfriend's birthday is one week away and you still don't know what to buy her. Well, you had better act fast if you want to avoid a swift kick to the testicles.

YEAR 1

Ask yourself how long you have been together. If you've only just started going out, play it safe. Be flirtatious and fun. **A 'Stay Over Kit' with pyjamas, toiletries and her favourite CD** (unless her music taste causes you sleepless nights of worry) is a good start, as is a pampering pack including moisturizer, soap, scented candles and the offer of a massage from you – yes, you! Cuddly toys, flowers and chocolates are a last resort, but she won't care how little you've spent if the presentation's right. If you're really struggling for inspiration, ask her best friend if she's dropped any hints about what she'd love.

The same can't be said if you've been together for over a year. No, sir. She's going to want to see not just the thought but the hard cash you've put into the gift. A nice piece of jewellery isn't enough on its own, so combine it with her birthstone or matching earrings. **A night in a hotel or a weekend away** will put a smile on her face – and yours – and framed art and perfume (bottled, not framed!) is always a winner too. One last word of warning: avoid clothes. Unless you want the words, 'But darling, I don't think you're frumpy … or fat' to become your catchphrase for the year.

YEAR 2

Survival guide to living at home with the folks

*What with **Soccer Saturday**, homemade shepherd's pie and fabric-softener-smooth boxer shorts, KIPPERS – Kids In Parents' Pockets Eroding Retirement Savings – have it made. That is, until the day they walk in on their folks having it off on the kitchen table. In an instant the dream is gone. Blasted to smithereens by a little pill called Viagra and a dusty old Barry White album.*

Here's how to live with the parents and still be your own man:

---

* Live independently in their home, buy your own food and offer to pay rent.

* Keep your self-respect, focus and drive. It sounds like something your dad might say, but just because you're staying in the same room you did as a kid doesn't mean you have to act like one.

* Don't be lazy. Your mum might not mind you hogging the sofa and remote all day long in nothing but your boxers, but soon enough your dad will make your life a living hell. Pick a chore to do daily – tidy the kitchen for example, take the bins out, empty the dishwasher – something your dad will notice and he won't have to do when he or your mum get in from work.

* Use the opportunity wisely. If you're moving back after a graduation or break up, set a time limit of six months to a year. Find a job, save some money and think about your next move in life.

* Accept your circumstances. A lack of independence and a feeling of emasculation can make meeting a lady friend problematic. But if you do, be upfront about your situation. Invite her over and introduce her to the folks. Don't tell them to bugger off out for the night (unless she's bringing a buxom blonde mate along for your dad, in which case you better book your mum into the local Travelodge).

* Respect your parents. Don't lie about playing your Xbox in your room all day. Integrate your parents into your life. Eat with them; go out with them and generally treat them like flatmates.

* Talk to your parents. If you feel like your folks are still treating you like a kid, sit them down and tell them so. Don't forget your parents were young once and they'll have some pearls of wisdom you'll never learn about if you never ask.

How to give yourself a number one cut

Step 1. Buy some quality clippers.

Step 2. Use two mirrors – one at the front, one at the back. Once you're confident enough you can switch to one.

Step 3. Pop the clippers on to grade one or two and shave all over.

Step 4. Fancy the Bic look? Wet your head all over or take a quick shower before you wield the razor.

Step 5. Apply some shaving oil or gel attentively – the more you work the foam in, the better the shave and the less sore your bonce.

Step 6. Shave the areas of little hair or light fluffy hair first. Save the coarser areas until last.

Step 7. Go slow and smoothly with the grain, letting the shape of your head dictate the path of the razor.

Step 8. When you're finished, wash your head with some soap and water and pat it dry with a towel. Apply a moisturizer to your head, preferably one with aloe vera or vitamin C, as alcohol-based ones can dry your scalp.

Step 9. You'll have to shave your head roughly every three days.

Step 10. **Don't forget to apply a high-factor sunscreen in summer – or wear a hat. Nothing worse than a bright red and painful bald head.**

The perfect fry-up

If you've ever experienced the sweet taste of a perfect fry-up you can give yourself a pat on the back – you are one of the breakfast elite, my friend. If you haven't, here's how to give yourself the treat of a lifetime. Ditch the Weetabix and listen up.

Set the oven to 200°C. Roll three good quality sausages in some oil and place them on a big baking tray next to a couple of frozen hash browns. Put the tray in the oven. Slice some mushrooms, cut a tomato in half and cut two pieces of bread into halves. Fry some bacon in a little oil in a big frying pan over a medium heat. While this is cooking, get a small saucepan, add a knob of butter and cook the mushrooms over a low heat. Put the tomato halves in with the bacon and wait for it all to cook. Remove and put aside. Dip the pieces of bread in the oil left over from the bacon. Fry all four pieces on a medium heat and turn once one side is crispy. The sausages and hash browns should be done by now, so put the bacon and tomatoes onto the baking tray and move it to the bottom shelf of the oven. Once the fried bread is done add it to the baking tray and turn the oven off.

Advanced tip:

The traditional Ulster Fry offers subtle variations. Try some fried potato bread, a fried Scotch pancake or fried soda bread as an alternative to plain white sliced.

Add a dessertspoonful more oil to the frying pan and wait until it sizzles, then break two eggs into it, spooning oil onto the yolks every now and then. Finally, plate up the rest of the food, add the eggs on top of the bread, pour yourself a cuppa and relax. Serve with brown sauce or ketchup to taste.

How to test for testicular cancer

The phrase 'I know it like the back of my hand' should, for this instance at least, be replaced with 'I know it like the back of my scrotum.' If you're going to safeguard against testicular cancer, you're going to have to familiarize yourself with your balls.

Get naked and have a look. Look in the mirror too. Notice how one ball differs from the other, observing which hangs lower or is larger. Now have a feel and note their usual weight and shape. This is the key to noticing any major differences in the future. Check them once a month after a warm bath or shower. Lift your right leg onto something like the sink – bathroom not kitchen – and gently cup your right testis in the hand you don't write with. Then, using your other hand, roll your ball between your thumb, forefinger and index finger. Swap legs and do the left testis. You'll notice a soft bump at the top and back of each testis: this is a tube called the epididymis. Other than these two bumps there should be no lumps or swellings. However, if you think you have found a hard, bone-like lump don't panic. First of all compare it with the other testis – it's very rare for cancer to develop in both testicles at the same time. If there isn't a similar-feeling lump in the same place make an appointment with your doctor and he'll check it for you. If you're feeling shy about this, don't be. A doctor has seen a lot of men's meat and two veg so he's not going to take one look at yours and laugh. However, if he does laugh he's probably not a doctor and you should zip up and leave the 'Doctor's Surgery' right away.

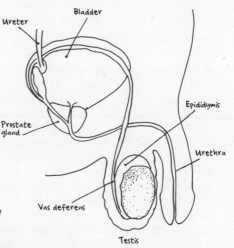

How to stay alive when you go shopping with the lady in your life

Women are programmed to find shopping displays fascinating. From nylon tights to diamond slippers they can't resist a little browse here, a little gander there. But when she picks up a pair of shoes you know she wouldn't wear in a month of half-price Mondays, feel free to show your impatience ... but only if you want to spend the night on the sofa with a packet of frozen peas hugging your nether regions.

At times, being the shadow-boyfriend is essential. When her face becomes ingrained with the look of intense shopping contemplation, stand well back. If interrupted at this point, she could hit out. Once she's picked out her clothes she'll want your opinion. At this juncture you need to remain as calm and appeasing as a peace envoy to the Middle East. Never lead with 'You look ...' Always blame the clothes or brand. 'That skirt doesn't look ...' etc. Be confident and positive in your answer. Too nonchalant and she'll think you don't care, too involved and she'll think you're trying to mould her into a Barbie doll. Keep it simple. 'That looks lovely on you' is spot on. Never say, 'Jesus love, you look like Michael Ball in *Hairspray*.'

At sales time, enlist a fellow couple on your mission. You boys can wander off and have a pint while the girls catfight over who saw the half-price cork wedges first. Alternatively, wander off on your own, but arrange to meet her back in *her* shop after half an hour or so.

It takes men five minutes to make a decision on an item of clothing. The same decision can take women five millennia. For this very reason, NEVER agree to a shopping trip with more than two women at a time. For each additional woman, add another hour on to each decision made. Be warned, however, no action beyond an arson attack – and even that's questionable – will speed a woman up. Patience and tact are your only tools. Despite the fact that every daintily hung belt is becoming a possible noose at this point, offer to play packhorse and carry her bags. At five o'clock, she'll show mercy on you and you'll be back in time for the footie results.

How to get rid of sweaty armpits before a big meeting

Armpits can smell fear. They pick up the scent of trepidation and pounce on it. Their aim: to send the new CEO running from the office, mentally scarred from the sight of sweat patches the size of saucers and the whiff of body odour redolent of rabid camel.

Here's how to banish the sweat monster before that important meeting:

Dress to suppress the sweat. When the last shake of the antiperspirant can or the final smear of the roll-on isn't enough, you're going to have to disguise the problem. A black or white shirt will go some way to conceal the patches, but as an extra protection, wear a high-quality cotton vest or undershirt to soak up any perspiration, leaving your shirts bone dry and sweat-patch free. Always wear loose cotton or linen shirts to allow the air to pass between your clothes and your body. Invest in a light linen suit for summer.

Avoid coffee, drink lots of water, and don't power-walk to work. Leave plenty of time to get to your meeting so you don't have to rush or panic. Keep your body temperature low, reduce the amount of heat your body gives off or receives.

Take off your jacket and loosen your collar and tie on the way there.

Take two shirts to work. Nip off shortly before the meeting starts and change in the gents. As for the odour, carry a little stick of body spray in your pocket or buy one specifically for your desk at work.

In severe cases, dab cider vinegar on your armpits before you go to bed, and wash them thoroughly in the morning. Drink a cup of green tea at night, as this dries your body oils up. Avoid spicy foods and alcohol. Carry a hand fan and cool yourself down at regular intervals.

Some home remedies you can try:

Drink sage tea instead of your usual brew.

Dust your oxters with bicarbonate of soda – it absorbs the sweat and acts as a deodorant.

Add two cupfuls of tomato juice to your bathwater and soak the pits for at least 15 minutes.

Drink a cup of tomato juice every day. You can do this while you soak in your tomato-juice bath.

Slice a potato, and rub the juice on your armpits, then apply deodorant as usual.

Extreme measures:

Lift your arms in front of the hand driers in the toilets every hour.
Have an auxiliary Botox injection pre-meeting.

Blagger's guide to internet chat room slang

We've come a long way from telegrams, smoke signals, and paper cups with string. Thanks to the internet, communication has never been so easy. If you're about to eat a packet of prawn cocktail crisps, you're only a click away from letting the world know on Facebook. With so much to say, and so little time to say it, heaven forbid Generation Instant Messenger should type twenty keys when only two will do.

Acronyms:

WUU2? = What you up to?

NM = Not much

LOL = Laughing out loud

ROFL = Rolling on the floor laughing

FOCL = Fall off chair laughing

LMAO = Laughing my ass off

PMSL = Pissing myself laughing

WTGP? = Want to go private?

FYI = For your information

GR&D = Grinning, running and ducking

IMO = In my opinion

AAR = At any rate

AFK = Away from keyboard

BAK = Back at keyboard

F2F = Face to face

ASL or a/s/l = Age, sex, location

IOW = In other words

AFAIK = As far as I know

JAS = Just a second

GAL = Get a life

LTNS = Long time no see

NIMBY = Not in my back yard

GBTW = Get back to work – one for the boss

OTW = On the way – file sent

PMJI = Pardon me for jumping in

BRB = Be right back

TTTT = These things take time

SOTA = State-of-the-art

TRDMF = Tears running down my face

FITB = Fill in the blanks

TTFM = Ta-ta for now

POS = Parents over shoulder

WTF = What the f**k?

ADIH = Another day in hell

ADIP = Another day in paradise

NIFOC = Naked in front of computer – often responded to with TMI, too much
information

BOFH = Bastard operator from hell

PTKFGS = Punch the keys for God's sake

FOAF = Friend of a friend

JK = Just kidding

KISS = Keep it simple stupid

MTFBWY = May the force be with you

NSFW = Not safe for work

MUSH = Multi-user shared hallucination

MYOB = Mind your own business

PITA = Pain in the arse

SOHF = Sense of humour failure

TANSTAAFL = There ain't no such thing as a free lunch

OMG = Oh my God

ZOMG = Zoh my gawd – a way of mocking those that use OMG all the time

JC = Just chilling

YAA = Yet another acronym

Random symbols:

XOXO = Hugs and kisses – one for the girlfriend

^5 = High five

?^ = What's up?

_/? = Cup of tea?

Emoticons:

Sideways faces showing emotions following the guidelines:

Colon = Eyes
Semi-colon = Winking eyes
Brackets = Lips
Hyphen = Nose. some cyber-rebels kick cyber civilization to the curb and don't even bother with a nose. Crazy. And they said the internet wouldn't change a thing

;-)~~~~~ = Giving someone raspberries

:-) = Smile

;-) = Wink

:-/ = Perplexed

:-(= Sad – probably because they don't have any friends. Real ones at least

:,-(= Crying

;-0 = Shouting

:-D = Big grin

<:-| = Curious – because all curious people obviously wear paper sailor hats

:-o = Surprised

:-| = Bored

:-X = Keeping mouth shut

;-)~ = Drooling, drunk or massive seizure

;-P = Sticking tongue out

;-{) = Someone with a moustache

8-) = Wearing glasses or being clever – in short, being a smartarse

Toolbox essentials

A good tradesman never blames his tools. But as you're a DIY amateur, inserting profanities before naming each tool is an essential part of your duty. Here's a must-have list for your f**king toolbox.

1. *A heavy claw hammer with a wooden handle.*

2. *Three varying sizes of Phillips screwdrivers*

3. *A flat-head screwdriver.*

   A cross-point screwdriver – a two-in-one screwdriver will suffice.

   Screws – all types and sizes.

4. *Needle-nose pliers – cutting and gripping pliers, also called 'snipe-nose' or 'pinch-nose' pliers. Handy for reaching awkward cavities where wires can't be reached with your fingers.*

5. *A medium-size wrench.*

6. *Retractable tape measure with lock feature.*

7. *Cordless or electric drill.*

8. *Angle square.*

9. *9" torpedo spirit level.*

   Pencil or chalk.

10. *Small hacksaw.*

   Old toothbrush.

   Nails.

11. *Putty knife.*

12. *Utility knife with blades that can be replaced.*

   Electric current detector.

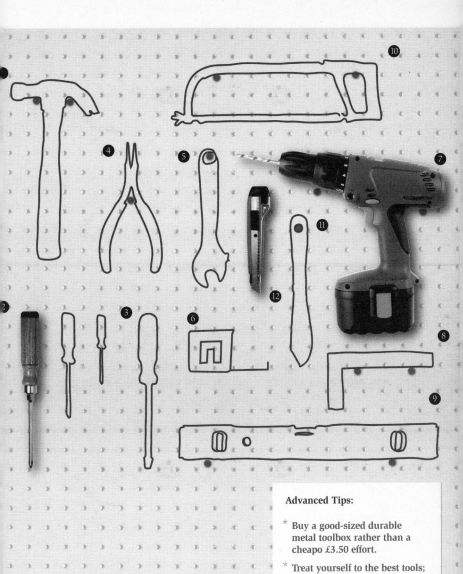

Advanced Tips:

* Buy a good-sized durable metal toolbox rather than a cheapo £3.50 effort.

* Treat yourself to the best tools; fork out at the start and make savings in the long run.

* Get some safety glasses for the more dangerous jobs.

How to give the perfect best man's speech

Winston Churchill might have been a great orator, but he is not a great role model for your first public speech. After all, you don't want to send the wedding guests or business partners to the buffet with a war cry echoing inside their heads.

Follow these guidelines and you won't have a riot on your hands:

Order:

* Have a funny opening line; a cocky icebreaker that sets all the guests at ease, but also lets them know this might be a little embarrassing for the groom.

* Point out some things about the wedding – be positive, don't say the food is rubbish and the service stinks.

* Set out your feelings about being best man. If you're a confident sort make a show of being nervous and vice versa. Send yourself up, but let everyone know you're in control.

* Give some hilarious and/or touching insights into your relationship with the groom.

* Lead into a character assassination – but don't be nasty or cruel. If he was still a virgin at 33 don't share this with the assembled guests.

* Mention the impact the new wife has had on your best mate's life. Be positive! Crying into your beer because she wouldn't let him come to the pub last Thursday shouldn't be mentioned. He'll have told you what she means to him – now's the time to let everyone else know.

* This is the bit you've been dreading – the honest appraisal and moving tribute to marriage. No matter what your views, congratulate the bride and groom on their nuptials and wish them all the best for the future.

*   Finish on a sincere or humorous, but not offensive, note. Whatever you do, don't wink at the bride's mother and make an overt sexual advance. Wait until the disco gets going for that.

*   *Raise a toast to the happy couple.*

Advice:

*   Don't get pissed before the speech.

*   Be open and talk frankly about the couple, but don't embarrass them. If they're looking uncomfortable change tack and move on to something else. It's their wedding not your debut stand-up show at the Comedy Store.

*   Thank the parents of both the groom and the bride – add extra thanks to the bride's dad for getting a decent amount of booze in and guarantee him you won't be letting any go to waste.

*   Balance out your speech, don't just witter on about the groom, know your stuff about the bride too.

*   An original and apposite quotation can be worked into the speech to either humorous or dramatic effect, but avoid clichés and anything too obvious, or you'll fall flat on your face.

*   Write out notes for your speech on the back of some cards. Use the notes to keep you on track, but engage your audience by making eye contact in a charming manner.

*   Speak slowly and calmly; don't rush in a nervous desire for it to be all over. Breathe and remember to smile as you speak. Before you know it you'll be back in your seat with a crescendo of applause ringing around your ears.

How to get rid of shaving cuts in a hurry

* Run a flannel under very hot water for a few minutes and press it on the offending bleeder.

* Press sugar or salt onto the cut to stop the bleeding.

* Apply some Vaseline to the spot. It won't heal it but it will stop it bleeding.

* Push a piece of toilet paper onto the cut; let some blood soak up into the tissue so it sticks. Leave for ten minutes, remove and the cut should have clotted. Remember to remove tissue before you leave the house.

* Press an ice cube against the cut to make the capillaries constrict and stop the bleeding.

* Spray some deodorant on your fingertip and press onto the cut. The aluminium compounds cause blood to clot more quickly.

* Dab some urine on your face. Shaving cut or smelling of pee? That's a tough one.

How to beat that Monday morning hangover from hell

With a brain feeling like the victim of a sensory deprivation chamber saboteur and a stomach doing the hokey-cokey, hangovers make Monday mornings even moodier. The main culprit of a hangover is a toxic chemical called acetaldehyde, the by-product of alcohol metabolism and breakdown. This chemical works on your brain and makes you sweat and feel nauseous.

The headache comes from your brain rattling around your head. Because all the cerebrospinal fluid (the stuff that your brain likes to take a dip in) has been sucked out to replenish your dehydrated body. What a lovely image.

The trick to preventing a hangover is to do all you can the night before the morning after arrives. The problem is that you are usually too drunk to remember what you should do.

Before you go drinking:

1. Take two tablespoons of olive oil and eat a baked potato before leaving the house. This will line the stomach.

2. Alternatively, swallow some milk thistle tablets. They help the liver deal with serious alcohol consumption and can help reduce after-effects.

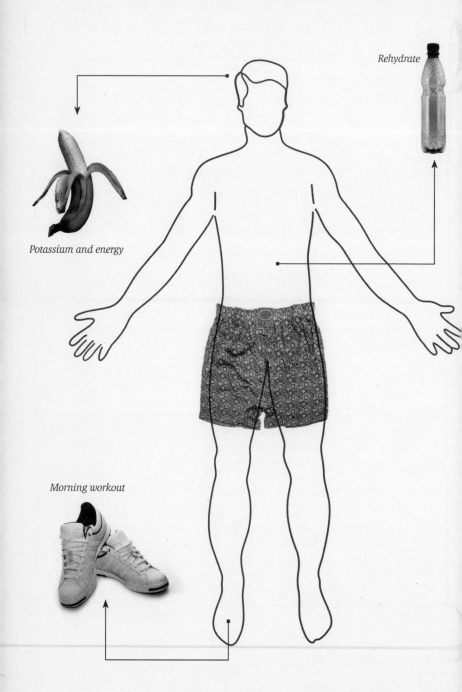

Rehydrate

Potassium and energy

Morning workout

Prairie Oyster recipe

- A Traditional Hangover Remedy -

2 dashes of white wine or malt vinegar
1 egg yolk
1tsp Worcestershire sauce
1tsp tomato ketchup
Black pepper

Directions:

Mix the vinegar, Worcestershire sauce and tomato ketchup in a glass. Separate the egg and carefully add the yolk to the glass, taking care that it doesn't break. Grind in some fresh black pepper.

Down in one go.

The hangover from hell sent straight back from whence it came!

Later, after the drinking session:

3. You should try necking pint after pint of water just before you collapse. This will help you rehydrate and prevent a devastating headache the next morning.

4. Some swear by Diarolyte, a diarrhoea remedy which helps to rehydrate and restore mineral salt and sugar levels in the body. Drink a sachet with water before bed.

If you still wake up with the head-bangers and the need to vomit:

5. Acetaldehyde's nemesis is cysteine, which can be found in eggs, meat and honey. So, if you can face it, a poached egg on toast, or, even better, the full fry-up, is the perfect remedy.

6. Try the traditional *Prairie Oyster recipe*.

7. Other cures include eating bananas, lemons and limes. These will settle your stomach and give you carbohydrates and potassium, which give you energy.

8. Tomato and orange juice boost your body's vitamin C as well as helping replace lost electrolytes.

9. A nice long hot shower, or a trip to the local steam room and sauna will revitalize your skin and help you sweat out the evil toxins.

10. A morning workout banishes toxins from your body and increases circulation which gets essential oxygen to your brain.

11. Pulling your hair gets blood to your head, reducing your headache and getting you some funny looks on the bus to work.

12. Beware the caffeine monster. Coffee will dehydrate you even more.

First date survival guide

Playground romance had its charms. A 'first date' consisted of a quick squeeze behind the bike shed, commemorated with a chorus of K-I-S-S-I-N-G from your mates. And once you'd written her initials in Tippex on your pencil case, you were as good as married. Out of the playground things get a little trickier. Show up to a date with a bottle of Tippex and a map to the nearest bike shed and the only thing you'll be kissing is the tears on your pillow.

Here's how to survive the first date:

The time and the place.

Gigs, the theatre or a film are all good but there's one problem: none involve talking. You'll want to get to know her in a relaxed environment where you can work your charms without distractions.

Go for a drink or a meal before the gig or film. You can calm those first-date nerves with a couple of pints, or if the outlook is grim, get hammered.

Mid-week is the best time for a first date.

If you're picking her up, knock twice, take a step back and look around outside. Don't stare dead ahead and wait for the door to open; don't bang on the door and shout, 'Come on darling. Get a f**king move on!'

Make eye contact. You don't want to look like a shifty weirdo.

Give her a light kiss on both cheeks, like a real Casanova.

Don't grab her hand the minute she's out the front door. She'll think you're possessive, or soppy. Or that you're taking sniper fire.

Pay her a compliment to set the tone – tell her she's looking lovely or amazing, or admire her dress.

First impressions.

Take a shower beforehand and arrive clean-shaven or with decent designer stubble.

Clean your teeth. Twice.

Dress to impress, but if you don't normally wear a suit and tie during the day, now is not the time to start. Just wear what you normally do when you go out on the town – some decent jeans, an ironed shirt and a jacket. Sometimes a T-shirt and pullover will look good if you look the part.

Give yourself plenty of time so you're not late and flustered. You'll already be sweating profusely so don't exacerbate the situation by running for the bus or your crotch area will feel like someone's just poured a jug of water on it.

Relax. Tell yourself you're just two good friends hanging out. So what if you goof up and make a fool of yourself? Women like men who can laugh at themselves; if you're too serious she'll have wished she'd stayed in with a good book.

Women like strong-looking men. Keep your back straight and your shoulders broad and don't slump over your pint (or curry if you're eating).

Be a gentleman, but don't go over the top. Hold the door open for her, buy the first round of drinks, and possibly pay for the meal, but don't refuse if she offers to pay half.

Conversation.

Don't bang on about yourself. Mentioning your job and where you grew up is one thing, describing in slow-mo the bicycle-kick equalizer you scored at the weekend is quite another.

Before you go out think about some topics you feel confident talking about. If there's an awkward silence – and there is always an awkward silence – nip into your memory bank and pull out a topic you prepared earlier.

Get the balance right between aloof and interested. Be playful and flirtatious and a little elusive at times. Don't give her every morsel of information; it's up to her to find out about you. Ah, the thrill of the chase.

Let her do some of the legwork. Smile when she's talking and let her finish before speaking.

Enjoy yourself. Even if the conversation is mundane consider that she might be bored too, so change tack and talk about something else.

Banter is good. Let her know you'll give as good as you get, but don't be afraid to let her have the last word.

Be confident but not overbearing. Don't be afraid to show weakness or ignorance on certain subjects. And if she's the intellectual type, don't pretend to have read the whole of Proust in the original French if you haven't.

Avoid religion, politics, money, sex, the ex or how children should be raised. Leave these until the fourth or fifth date.

Look at her, not at the hot waitress who keeps brushing past your table.

Pick up on her body language. Open palms towards you, shoulders lifted and leaning towards you and smiling at you while looking into your eyes are all signs she doesn't find you repellent.

At the end of the night.

Walk or drive her home if you live nearby. Even if the date has gone badly and you pretty much want to vomit when you make eye contact it is common courtesy to make sure the lady gets home safely.

Wait for her to go indoors before you either walk away or drive off, but don't loiter about staring up at her bedroom window.

If she's played with her hair, kept up eye contact and sounded interested and giggled with you – not at you – generally speaking she's enjoyed your company and wouldn't turn down an innocent kiss. If it turns into a full-on snog, that's a bonus, but she'll admire your gentlemanly restraint. Leaving her wanting more is much better than a face full of mace.

If she asks you if you fancy coming in for a coffee, she actually genuinely means a coffee despite what your friend in your pants is telling you. Stripping down to your underpants when she pops into the kitchen to put the kettle on will scare the living daylights out of her.

When saying goodbye, only say you'll call her if you really want to.

How to sell your car

*Between rolling out of the showroom to death in a scrap-yard
a million miles from home, a car will have many owners.
Some will put their feet up on the dashboard, some will cut
off the feet of those who dare. All will shed a tear when the
day comes to say goodbye.*

Here's a step-by-step guide to selling your car:

Step 1. Know the market. Family cars are always in demand because – yes,
you guessed it – people are always having babies. 4x4s will be easier to
sell in the countryside. Convertibles and sports cars in the summer. Vans
will always sell at competitive prices due to the never-ending evolution of
the apprentice. But collector cars will have particular buyers.

Step 2. Price your car. Check the ads in *Auto Trader,* local newspapers and
used car websites. Note the mileage, condition and price. How many other
cars like yours are on the market? Work out a realistic value of your car and
add on a couple of hundred quid for good measure.

Step 3. Make your car buyable. Dents, scrapes, and ex-girlfriend's key
markings should all be taken care of prior to sale. Get a close friend to
take the car for a test drive; they can often hear any unusual noises that
you have got used to. A mechanic can then give your car a once-over and
give you a report. You can either pay for what he suggests – and keep the
receipt to show the buyer – or factor it into the price, informing the buyer
of what extra work needs to be done.

Step 4. Spruce it up. First impressions are crucial. Take the car to a good
hand car wash and pay for a valet clean, or do it yourself. Properly. Don't
forget to wipe the dashboard with polish cleaner, empty the ashtrays and
vacuum the carpet thoroughly. Make sure the V5 logbook and latest MOT
certificates along with owner's and stereo manuals are all in the glove
compartment. Top up all fluids. Check the spare, jack and all the light
bulbs. Remove old copies of the *Sun* strewn across the back seat and the
pair of pants dangling from the gear stick.

Step 5. Sell to a local dealership. It can be the perfect solution if you don't
have time to go through the whole rigmarole of advertising and viewings.
Garages offer roughly 20% less than the actual value of the car – that's

how they make their profit. However, a garage might be the best way to go, if you know your car needs repairs. Less money but also less hassle.

Step 6. Advertise. Newspapers ads cost £30 or so, online ads £15. Online ads include more space for photos and information and also reach a wider audience. However, research the company first so you know they're not pulling a fast one and remember to read the small print. Noticeboards in local shops, word of mouth and parking your car at a decent location, e.g. outside a university with a sign in the window, are also options. Your ad must include: year, model, make, colour, number of owners, automatic or manual, mileage and condition.

Some selling slang:

* **Must sell** – your price is low because you're getting out of town.

* **OBO** – 'Or best offer.' Lets punters know you're open to negotiation.

* **Asking price** – you'll waver a little on the price but not by much.

* **Firm** – no rush to sell. You'll wait for the right buyer.

* **As is** – the car will be sold as it is with no further repairs done.

Step 7. Viewing. Once the ad is placed, be ready to receive calls. If you answer the phone half-cut and slurring over prices the person on the other end is hardly going to feel comfortable going on a test drive with you, let alone be happy to buy your car. Be friendly, polite, interested and accommodating. Answer any questions honestly and if they want a test drive check their driving licence and accompany them. A request for their mechanic to give the car a once-over is acceptable as long as you don't have to pay for the service. If you doubt their integrity, refuse. Last but not least, sell the car. Point out all bonus features – CD player, electric windows, your extensive collection of Page 3 clippings, etc.

Step 8. Negotiate. Know your lowest acceptable price and stick to it. Use the punter's eagerness to push them to the price you're looking for. Don't rush the sale. Be willing to wait for a few viewings so you get the right price. However, if you get what you're looking for first time out, do the deal. If you don't get any buyers at all, be ready to drop your price to a more realistic one, you greedy git.

Step 9. Finalizing the sale. Shake hands and organize the transfer of funds. If they want to pay by cheque, be polite but say you'll have to wait for it to clear before you let them have the car – if they say no they're trying to pull one. Check the car once more to make sure you haven't left any prize magazines in the boot and record the mileage on the dial. If the car breaks down after the sale you are not legally bound to accept responsibility, however it is common courtesy to try and fix the problem if the breakdown occurs on your driveway.

Step 10. Documentation. Notify the DVLA of the sale by using the V5C (V5C/3) part of the registration certificate – if you're selling to a dealership. If you've lost the certificate, you can order a new one from the DVLA website. You can also inform the DVLA by sending them a letter with the date of sale, model, make and the name and address of the new driver. The new driver will also need to inform the DVLA in writing. If you don't officially inform them that the car has changed hands, you're still liable for tax or penalties accrued by the new driver. You should receive acknowledgement from the DVLA within four weeks. Keep a record of the buyer's name, phone number and address. Cancel your insurance.

How to build a campfire
like a Boy Scout

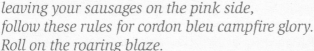

If you've never had the sensation of biting into a half-cooked sausage you've never lived. Or nearly died of food poisoning, more like. So if your attempts at building a campfire result in a dwindling flame, leaving your sausages on the pink side, follow these rules for cordon bleu campfire glory. Roll on the roaring blaze.

Choose an area with no overhanging branches that's shielded from the wind. Next, forage for wood. Avoid green or wet wood. The rule of thumb for the perfect fire is DEAD BUT STILL ON THE TREE. The wood will be perfectly dry and will burn magnificently for cooking.

To start a fire, you need to collect:

* **Tinder** – Twigs, shavings, strips of dry bark (birch is perfect), dry leaves, grass and thistle tops. This forms the base of the fire which burns quickly and ignites the larger pieces of wood.

* **Kindling** – Thin, small and very dry sticks about 30cm long. When properly placed, these keep the fire alive while allowing oxygen to enter.

* **Fuel** – Larger pieces of dry dead wood and little logs, along with some green or live wood. The live wood is wet with sap and is slower burning than the dead wood, giving a well-balanced fire. This wood fuel makes for a long-burning and enduring fire.

Tip:

To keep your fire alight overnight, simply remove all large logs which are still burning to the edge of the fire. Cover the glowing embers with ash, then carefully pile large stones over the top. Next morning, remove the stones (caution: they might be hot enough to fry an egg), add fresh kindling and logs from the edge of the fire. And *voilà!*

Now it's time to build.

* If the ground is wet, lay a base using lengths of green or live wood.

* Grab a handful of tinder and ball it together to form a nest at the centre of your chosen area. Place some kindling on top in the form of a tepee, or pyramid, making sure to leave gaps for the fire to breathe. Poke some birch strips or dry bracken in among the kindling to help it catch. Next, place four kindling sticks in a square around the tepee, followed by five or six sticks on top of them, to create a miniature wooden fence. Place two larger pieces of dry wood on opposite sides and build a partial roof of wood fuel, propping up the sticks between the fire and the wood with clumps of tinder.

* Sit with the wind on your back and light the fire by poking a match through a gap. Light the tinder first and the flames should spread to the tepee, the fence and finally the larger pieces of wood on top. Long, slow blows from the depths of your lungs will keep the fire ignited, as will adding the remnants of your forage.

* Let the fire die down to an even flame, with lots of smouldering embers, then prepare your cooking pan and let the sausage sizzle commence. Anyone for a round of 'Kumbaya'?

Getting the most out of being the designated driver

Whether you're stood stone-cold sober in the middle of the dance floor surrounded by strangers screeching Robbie William's 'Angels', or cowering in the corner trying to avoid the advances of a Saga subscriber, one orange juice-fuelled-evening is often enough to make you wish you'd never passed your driving test.

However, there are ways to make those Saturday nights of sobriety a little bit more bearable. First of all, rule with an Iron-Bru fist. Be firm, and don't put up with any nonsense. You're saving your friends countless pennies on the taxi ride home, so it's not entirely unreasonable if you want to leave a good half an hour or so before the bright white lights scatter the revellers like vampires at dawn.

After midnight, things usually get messy, so make the most of your friends' company at the start of the evening; get them to pay for your alcohol-free cocktails and enjoy yourself. Being sober doesn't mean you can't joke or flirt. In fact, turn it to your advantage. Let's face it, not punctuating every sentence with a belch enhances your chances of scoring rather than limits them. Stepping in to 'rescue' a damsel in distress from one of your drunken mates' loutish slurring chat-up attempts will make you seem like a knight in shining armour. By comparison, prospective girlfriends will find you articulate and erudite. What's more, the promise not to redecorate the interior of her bathroom with Gastric Yellow, let alone freak her out of her skin by dancing like you're having some sort of fit, should (at the very least) get you a phone number or two by the end of the night.

The answer to the question: 'How much can I drink and still be under the limit?' is simple. Either don't drink at all or, if being seen in a bar brandishing anything but a beer is tantamount to walking down your local high street naked, two 275ml bottles of 4% lager spread out over the night, or a couple of pints of weak bitter shandy, will keep your dignity and faculties nicely intact. Tell the barman that you're the designated driver – this should guarantee your drinks are measured correctly and your pint of shandy won't send you and your car the wrong way down the high street. It will win you his sympathy and someone sober to talk to when the rest of your party become incoherent or preachy.

When closing time arrives, rounding everyone up can be tricky. Most stragglers will quicken their pace with a few short, sharp thwacks to the back of the thighs, but if you haven't got a bamboo cane to hand, shouting over the crowd that you're leaving, marching to your car and revving the engine like a 17-year-old at his first set of traffic lights normally spreads panic.

Once the cries of 'Shotgun!' have died down, feel free to overrule the verdict and elect the least drunk or most sleepy of your comrades to ride up front. Wind down the windows – a blast of good cold air could help hold any nausea among your passengers at bay.

As you approach the witching hour and the embers of the night begin to fade choruses of 'I love you' and 'You're a star, you are' will echo around your car like a stuck CD. This is the perfect time to drop a few hints about petrol money. Silence will ensue but soon enough the drink-induced guilt will kick in and you'll be showered with pound coins from every quarter of the car.

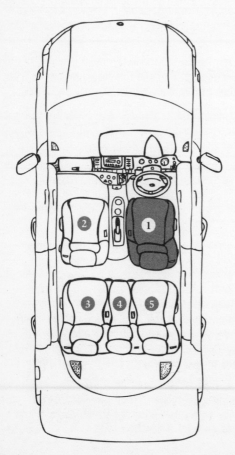

KEY

1. You
2. **Least drunk**
3. **Most drunk**
   (window down)
4. **Most chatty**
5. **Most sleepy**

How to do keepie uppies

How high up the latrine can you pee? How many bare breasts – your mum's don't count – have you seen? How many keepie uppies can you do in a row? The mark of a man on the playground is far from the mark of a man in the workplace. But when the boss challenges you to a freestyle soccer sesh, deploy these moves and he'll be running for the sanctuary of the girls' bathroom before you can say Ronaldinho.

The basics

Step 1. Pick a warm day to practise, pull on some board shorts or, if it's a particularly humid day, Speedos, and make sure you're on a flat surface.

Step 2. Drop the ball onto your favoured foot and kick it back from whence it came. Don't hoof it. Elevate your toes higher than your heel so the ball spins towards you and tap it about knee height in the air.

Step 3. Rather than trying to do twenty keepie uppies in a row straight off, concentrate at first on mastering a straight kick. Catch the ball, drop, kick, catch, drop, kick, catch, etc.

Step 4. Once you've perfected your balance and can kick the ball vertically, practise doing two keepie uppies in a row.

Step 5. Continue to practise until you can do five or six without the ball touching the ground.

Step 6. Now it's time to start with the ball at your feet. Put your favoured foot on top of the ball, quickly roll it back and, with the speed of Road Runner on heat, slip your foot behind it. As the ball rolls over your toe kick it up and start juggling.

Step 7. Mix it up with a bit of a knee or thigh action and switch feet once in a while. When you've done about fifty in a row you're a freestyle funkster.

Sussed the juggling? Try your hand at these advanced keepie uppie moves:

Around the world

The aim of the ATW is to knock the ball up slightly, circle it – hence the expression around the world – and then catch it on your toe before it touches the ground.

Step 1. Balance the ball on your favoured foot.

Step 2. Let the ball shift a little to the outside of your foot.

Step 3. As the ball begins to slide off your foot, lift your foot up the inside of the ball, over the top and down the other side. Don't brush the ball as you circle it.

Step 4. Catch the ball on your toe.

Rai Flick

This trick lifts the ball up and over your head. It's a great skill for flicking the ball over defenders on the pitch or old people in the park.

Step 1. As you dribble towards the defender, move your body over the ball.

Step 2. Clinch the ball between both feet and lift the ball up into the air. Attempt to flick the ball with one of your heels for added height.

Step 3. Run around the defender and control the ball on the other side.

Headstall

Not the best trick to pull off mid-game or you might get a mouthful of studs, but a classic to impress the ladies.

Step 1. Bend your neck so your face is towards the sky.

Step 2. Place the ball in the middle of your forehead just below your hairline.

Step 3. Keep your hand on the ball until it is balanced then peel your fingers away one by one.

Step 4. Relax your body, keep your eyes on the ball and use your neck and shoulder muscles to level out the ball's slight movements.

Blagger's guide to Texas Hold'em

Wild Bill Hickok. Gunfighter, professional gambler and all-round figurehead of the American Old West. In 1876 he was playing poker when a past loser shot him in the back of the head. Legend says Wild Bill was holding a pair of aces and a pair of eights at the time. The infamous Dead Man's Hand.

Old Wild West tales aside, assuming you've got at least four friends, here's how to have a go at stealing their pocket money:

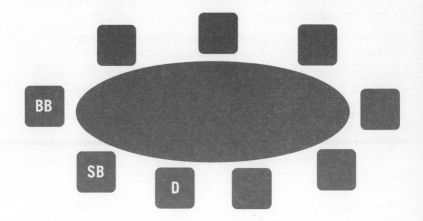

D = Dealer
SB = Small Blind
BB = Big Blind

The object of Texas Hold'em poker is to create the best five-card hand using any of the seven cards available. The two 'hole' cards which are dealt to each player at the start of the game and which only they can see and use. And the five cards which are dealt in the middle of the table throughout the game, called 'community' cards because they can be seen and used by everybody.

Step 1. Set a minimum and maximum bet, shuffle the cards and put on some smooth jazz.

Step 2. Use an empty beer can, ashtray, etc. to mark player 1, the dealer.

Step 3. Before the cards are dealt, the two people to the left of the dealer, player 2 and player 3, place 'blind' bets – so called because the players make them without seeing any cards. Player 2 bets the small blind, half of the lowest limit. Player 3 bets the large blind, the complete lowest limit.

Step 4. Each player is dealt two 'hole' cards – one at a time – face down on the table. The dealer receives the last card.

Step 5. Pre-flop round. Player 4 begins the betting round and betting continues clockwise round the table. Your options for each betting round are as follows:

* Call the bet – in the first round each player, bar player 3, must call the large blind bet to enter the game. In later rounds when calling the bet, a player must equal the previous amount of money placed in the pot. For example, player 3 raises the bet to £8, player 4 must therefore call the £8 to stay in the game or fold.

* Raise – place at least double the previous bet in the pot to up the stakes and put pressure on the other players. For example, a previous bet of £2 must be raised to £4 or more; bets can only increase, not decrease.

* Fold – opt out of the game. Give your cards back to the dealer due to a bad hand or a raise in the bet you're not willing to equal.

* Check – don't bet but stay in the game. Checking is not allowed on the first round because you must bet to enter the game. Each new round, once someone has raised the bet you can only call, raise or fold, not check.

Step 6. The first betting round ends with player 3 – although player 2 and 3 placed blind bets, these don't count as their official first bet: they are a way of ensuring each hand played has some money in the pot. However, if no one has raised the bet, player 3 can check without calling his original 'big blind' bet.

Step 7. It is important to note at this point that each betting round only ends when every player has either folded or called the largest bet. Rounds must end with everyone still in the game having an equal stake in the pot.

Step 8. The flop. The dealer deals the first three 'community' cards face up in the middle of the table.

Step 9. Another betting round begins from player 2, or, if player 2 has folded, the next player still in the game to the left of the dealer. This is the starting point for all subsequent betting rounds post-flop.

Step 10. At the end of that round a fourth community card, or the turn card is dealt.

Step 11. Play another round – in this and the next round the minimum bet is equal to double the large blind bet.

Step 12. The last community card, the river card is dealt.

Step 13. Final betting round.

Step 14. The showdown. All remaining players show their cards and the winning hand takes the cash in the pot. If only one person remains and all other players have folded, the last man standing scoops the pot.

Step 15. Move the dealer/player 1 marker clockwise one place and start another game.

Extra tips:

* Pennies, pounds or even matchsticks will suffice as chips if you don't want to bankrupt your best mates.

* You do not have to use both your hole cards when making your five-card hand.

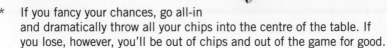

* If you fancy your chances, go all-in and dramatically throw all your chips into the centre of the table. If you lose, however, you'll be out of chips and out of the game for good.

* When all other players have folded by the showdown you do not have to reveal your hand; if you've won by a two pair, however, this is the time to gloat.

* The card ranking always determines the winner. The highest pair wins – two 7s trump two 5s, for example. The highest-ranking straight wins and the highest card at the end of the flush determines tied flushes.

* With regards to straights, cards cannot 'wrap' – go from Q, K, A, 1, 2, for example.

* If a game is tied, decide the winner with the 'kicker' card. This is the card next in line in your hand. It is common to use only one card in your hand to make a winning hand and therefore in the event of a tie,

use your second card as a kicker – if it is more than your opposition's kicker card you take the pot.

* In the rare occasion that ties cannot be determined – as sometimes happens with straights – divide the pot between all winners.

Poker Hands

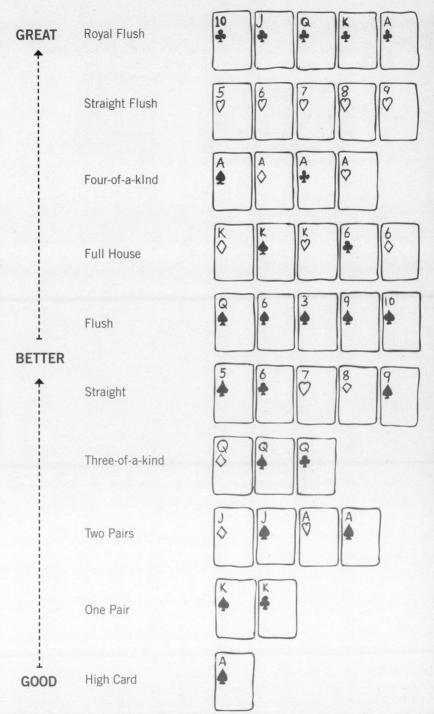

The Indispensable Bin Bag: A Rough Guide

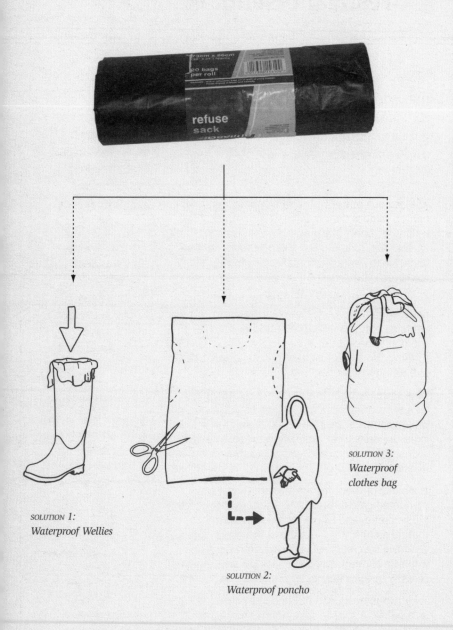

SOLUTION 1:
Waterproof Wellies

SOLUTION 2:
Waterproof poncho

SOLUTION 3:
Waterproof clothes bag

Festival essentials

As the summer sun rises and the days roll into one, it's only a matter of time before festival season arrives. The key to festival-going nirvana is to forget about fashion and concentrate on necessity.

The obvious ones first: tent, sleeping bag, clothes, lighter, large water container (full, obviously), wellington boots and/or old trainers, rainproof anorak, hat, money, sun lotion, penknife, condoms, torch, loo roll, Immodium tablets, toothpaste and toothbrush and wet wipes.

If you've still got room consider these: a battery-powered radio to keep the music going when the lights go out, some firewood and firelighters – so you don't spend three hours in a drunken haze rubbing two sticks together – and a cooking stove and pan for those morning fry-ups.

Take some bin bags; their uses are endless. Cut a hole for your head to make a poncho, use them as waterproof mats, wear them inside your wellies for extra-dry protection, wrap and tape them around your shoes or boots, and keep your spare clothes dry in one.

If it's one of those festivals where there is a monitored gate between the sleeping area and the music arena, and where there is security checking that no alcohol goes into the arena, make sure you have several small water bottles as big ones won't be allowed. You can sneak gin or vodka past security in the small water bottles.

Take two jumpers and put one in a pillowcase to use as a pillow. Also take something to make your tent stand out. A distinct flag from a rare country will work, but be prepared to meet some strange people. Mind you, that's what festivals are all about.

CHECKLIST

Essentials:

- ☐ Tent
- ☐ Sleeping bag
- ☐ Clothes
- ☐ Lighter
- ☐ Large water container
- ☐ Boots/old trainers
- ☐ Anorak
- ☐ Hat
- ☐ Money
- ☐ Sun lotion
- ☐ Torch
- ☐ Penknife
- ☐ Immodium tablets
- ☐ Condoms
- ☐ Loo roll
- ☐ Toothpaste
- ☐ Toothbrush
- ☐ Bin bags
- ☐ Wet wipes

Luxuries:

- ☐ Battery-powered radio
- ☐ Firewood/lighters
- ☐ Gas stove
- ☐ Frying pan

Tip: A few luxury items you might consider: anti-bacterial gel for washing hands, a shooting stick to lean on when everyone else is getting coated in muck, head-torch, hand-cranked phone charger, solar powered backpack with MP3 plug-in, tent locator and homing tag, and last but not least, spoil your girl with a Shewee which enables her to pee standing up.

How to negotiate a pay rise with the boss

In the current economic crisis, wading into your boss's office and demanding a pay rise will probably be met with arched eyebrows and incredulous laughter. But if you think you're worth more than you're earning, argue your point with sound judgement and provide adequate reasons. The corporate purse may spring open just for you.

Here's how to stake your claim for a seat on the gravy train.

Think about why you deserve a pay rise:

* How long have you been at your position? Have you taken on new responsibilities? Or trained new employees?

* Consider your value to the company. Be honest about what you're worth and what your boss will think you're worth.

* Gauge the 'supply and demand' of your position. If someone else could easily supply your skills the company won't pay you more to do something a chimp could do.

* Everyone moves up the rungs of the ladder; wait your turn, don't attempt to leapfrog others.

* Don't ask for a pay rise if others are being laid off. The best time to negotiate your salary is after you've been consistently working at a high level for several months and preferably when your department or company as a whole is not in decline.

Compile evidence to back up your claim:

* Research salary surveys online, question contacts in other companies, browse job advertisements and find the going market rate for your position.

* Write a list of any new responsibilities you have taken on since joining the company.

* List the skills which make you an important asset to the team. Awards and exceeded expectations should also be listed.

* Letters or emails of praise from colleagues – not including the doorman – or clients will back up your claims of importance.

* Consider your main accomplishments. Securing a new client, finalizing a deal or consistent sales all point towards an indispensable member of the team.

* Make sure your information is well presented and in a logical order.

Prepare yourself for the big showdown:

* Arrange a meeting with your direct line manager or boss. Under no circumstances go above your boss's head by going straight to his or her boss.

* Request a meeting either via his or her secretary or send an email. Say that you'd like a career review, rather than bluntly stating that the meeting is to ask for a pay rise.

* Plan what you want to say in advance. Make notes, and have a practice run with a close friend or partner. Don't tell everyone at your workplace you're going to 'milk the gaffer dry'.

* Set a clear objective in your head. Know what salary you would like and what you'd be willing to settle for. Give yourself room to negotiate within those boundaries.

* Prepare responses to any questions or concerns your boss may raise. Remember, he'll have to defend any pay increase to his or her boss as well.

* When you enter the office, thank your boss for making time to see you.

* Take a deep breath, don't enter into small talk or start to stutter. Be factual, professional and straight to the point and present all your information in a concise and articulate manner.

* Clearly state you're happy at the company and that you're not looking for a new job but you'd like to discuss your pay.

* Don't simply bombard your boss with stats, give brief examples of your achievements and hand over the documents you've prepared. If necessary, give your boss some time to think over and consider your case.

Negotiating and leaving with what you want:

* If your boss is open to your request for more pay, never start the bidding. Let them make the first move. Remain silent for at least 30 seconds after his first offer; this may provoke him or her to offer you more.

* On the other hand, if you are pushed to state a price, always ask for more than you actually expect – within reason. Don't ask for a million pounds in brand new notes.

* Take an active part in the discussion and be respectful of your boss's position. However, don't talk too much or you may end up agreeing to something you don't want.

* Negotiate. The final package may not incorporate money alone; your boss may want you to go on a training course or work extra hours. You could also ask for more holiday or take on more responsibilities – be flexible.

* Be friendly but in control. Don't come over all emotional and mention your need for a plasma telly in a flood of tears.

* If your request is declined on monetary reasons alone, ask your boss to review your pay at the next possible opportunity.

Blagger's guide to fishing

Man versus fish. The age-old battle. Homer Simpson vs General Sherman, the legendary and elusive 500lb catfish. Richard Dreyfuss and Co. vs Jaws senior. Ah, the thrill of the chase. A thrill the fish hardly experiences, having been hooked, whacked over the head with an oar and cooked on a red-hot skillet.

You will need:

Fishing rod and reel. You can buy these already strung with a line from fishing shops or department stores. Preferably the line should be 4–16 pound tested – how strong the line is, called poundage – and the rod medium light, between 5 and 6 feet long.

Bait. Bait and tackle shops are widely available in fishing areas. Choose worms for your first time; live bait is widely considered the best form of bait for fishing novices.

A pack of hooks. Size 6 covers most fish, unless you snare a Great White.

One or two bobbers or floats. Brightly coloured for easy observing.

Non-lead split-shot sinkers. Small weights to make sure the bait sinks and the line doesn't float on top of the water.

A friend. So you don't a) go mad from isolation, b) starve from male pride.

Bucket. To keep the fish in once caught.

Optional: *fishing net.*

Optional: *fishing knife.*

Sea fishing requires no licence whatsoever. Lake or river fishing requires a rod licence, which costs between £10 and £70. You may also need to pay for the right to use a landowner's body of water.

Step 1. Ask local fishing shops for tips on good fishing spots. Other anglers are likely to keep their special little places secret, so there's no point asking them.

Step 2. Tie the hook to the end of the rod (see page 130 for knots). Thread the hook all the way into the worm.

Step 3. Place the bobber or float on the line about 3 feet above your hook. And leave about 10 inches of line between the bobber and the tip of your rod.

Step 4. Clip a split-shot to your line slightly above the hook. Add more according to the conditions; strong currents require more weight than calm water.

Step 5. Set the drag on the reel. The drag is the amount of line that is released by the reel from the fish's end. Too tight and the line could snap, too loose and the hook might not catch the fish's mouth. As a general rule, set your drag to 25% of the line's poundage.

Step 6. Cast your line. Hold down the button on the reel. Keep your elbow still and draw the rod back until your hand is level with your ear and your wrist bent back at 2 o'clock. Quickly 'whip' the end forward and release the button as your forearm sticks out at 11 o'clock. Follow through to 10 o'clock. WARNING: make sure no one is behind you when you cast or you might end up hooking a human instead.

Step 7. Monitor the bobber and/or keep a finger rested on the line. You'll need to stay patient and relatively quiet. Metallica banging out on the radio isn't music to a fish's ears.

Step 8. When you feel tension on the line, the bobber or float submerge or drift away upstream slightly, a fish may well have fancied a nibble of your worm.

Step 9. To 'set' the hook in the fish's mouth jerk the rod back and up. If the line goes tight and starts to follow the movements of a fish you've got him.

Step 10. Once hooked the fish will start to fight like Rocky in round 12, so steady your grip, let him have some drag and lift the rod vertically – so your arms and rod take the brunt of his fisticuffs. Wait until he begins to tire, lower the rod to a 45° angle and reel him in until your rod is horizontal with the water. Lift and lower again and repeat. If he makes another run for it, lift and let him go. Once the drag stops coiling off, reel him in once more. Remember, always keep the line tight to ensure the fish doesn't shake off the hook.

Step 11. A net is handy at this point to catch the fish. If you haven't got one, grasp him by hand – be warned, many a fish has escaped the dinner plate due to slipping away, so cradle rather than grip.

Step 12. Once on shore, hold the fish away, avoiding the fins – they can be sharp – squeeze so its mouth opens to locate the hook. Look at the way it has gone in and try to 'back' it out in reverse – don't yank or you'll rip the fish's mouth.

Step 13. Decide whether to eat or free the fish. If it's a tiddler, it won't amount to more than a mouthful so show some mercy; slide the fish back into the water.

Step 14. If it's for the frying pan, kill the fish quickly. Do not leave it to suffocate. Hit it firmly at the back of head with a blunt instrument – the handle of your fishing knife should do the trick – and put it in a bucket of cold water.

Extra tips:

* If the fish are not playing ball, shut up shop and try another spot.

* Many beginners mistake the pull of the current for a bite; only over time and through trial and error will you be able to tell when a bite is a bite.

* If you're fishing for sport rather than for the plate, crush the barb of the hook with pliers so you can easily remove the hook from the fish's mouth without causing trauma.

* Research the area you plan to fish in. Some places have restrictions on live bait and others have restrictions on fishing itself.

* Check for knots in your line: they hamper your cast and weaken the line.

When to fish:

✔ Sun behind clouds – good

✔ Cloud – good

✔ Rain – good

✔ Warm front – good

✔ Light wind – good

✘ Hot sun – poor

✘ Thunderstorm – poor

✘ Cold front – poor

✘ No wind – poor

How to gut a fish

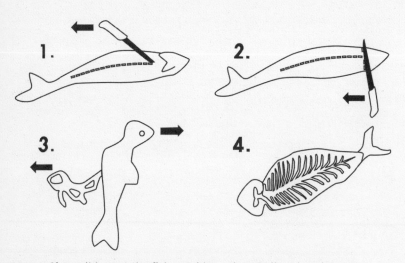

Step 1. If possible, gut the fish outside – the smell and scales get everywhere – or spread plenty of newspaper on the work surface.

Step 2. Rinse the fish thoroughly under cold running water.

Step 3. Remove the fins with a sharp knife or kitchen scissors.

Step 4. Descale the fish. Hold the fish at the head or tail; use a blunt knife, butter knife or the edge of a spoon and scrape from the tail towards the head at a 90° angle, using firm, quick strokes away from your body. Pay special attention to the gill area.

Step 5. Run your hand up from the tail end to check all scales are removed, then rinse the fish in cold, clean water.

Step 6. Place the fish belly up and use a small sharp knife to make a shallow cut from the soft bit of the belly near the tail to the gills. Don't insert the knife too deep or you'll split the guts open.

Step 7. Spread the cavity and pull out the entrails by grabbing the main connecting tissue at the base of the head and pulling it loose.

Step 8. Rinse inside and outside the fish.

Step 9. Remove the head behind the gills and the tail where it connects with the body.

Step 10. Plonk your fish on the grill or campfire.

How to dry your jeans in 15 minutes

Wet jeans. They cling to your legs like a superhero's spandex, smell of damp newspaper and have a crotch damper than a boy's pants on his first day at school. Whether you're running late for a date or just picking Mum up from bingo, here's how to get comfortably dry jeans in a jiffy.

Step 1. First of all, while your jeans are still in the wash you've got a bit of pantaloon preparation to do. Pinch your mum's or girlfriend's hairdryer, turn the central heating on – or at least one radiator – and whack the iron on its highest setting.

Step 2. Remove jeans from the washing machine. Turn jeans inside out, take outside and, gripping them firmly at the waist, give them good airing. Dash back into house. Grab your leather belt and place lengthwise on hot radiator.

Step 3. Plonk jeans on ironing board and run the hot iron over both front and back. Concentrate on the thicker areas – waistline, pockets, ankle cuffs and crotch. Press iron onto these sections and leave for a few seconds until they steam. If you smell burning you've overdone it.

Step 4. Turn jeans right side out and run iron all over again, front and back. Switch iron off and grab hairdryer. Crank hairdryer up to hottest and highest setting and push nozzle into either pocket. Rotate nozzle and blast crotch area with hot air for up to two minutes per pocket.

Step 5. Put jeans on – if not bone dry, they'll at least be nice and warm, in damp a way, especially round the waistline. Feed the hot belt through the loops and by the time you arrive at your destination your waistline will be warmer than toast.

Wet jeans? What wet jeans?

Coping with premature hair loss

For some, BALD is the ultimate four-letter word. But while losing your hair at an early age isn't a laughing matter, it isn't the end of the world. Here's how to deal with the early onset of hair loss.

Men can start to lose their hair from the age of 15 onwards. Some men are bald by the time they're 25, for others it can take up to 20 years. So, don't panic and shave your head at the first sign of hairs on your pillow or in the plughole. If you notice thinning or wispy hair, a receding hairline and/or a developing bald patch on the crown of the head, avoid using a hairdryer as it can damage your scalp, wash your hair every day to keep it healthy and lay off your dad's Just For Men.

If you do continue to lose your hair, and the balding makes styling problematic – comb-overs are a no-no – visit the barber and have your hair clipped really short, or buy some clippers and ask a friend to shave your head. With practice, you'll be able to use the clippers yourself. (Think of all the money you'll save on barbers and hair products.) Put all your worries about big ears and shiny pates to one side and embrace your new look.

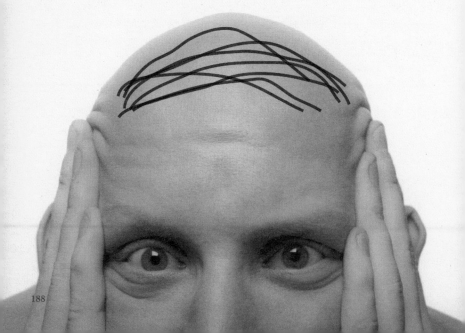

Look in the mirror, and think Thierry Henri, Samuel L Jackson, Andre Agassi and Bruce Willis. Not William Hague and the Pub Landlord. You may have changed on the outside and, as a man, lost one of your major areas of self-expression, but you're still the same gorgeous, sexy dude inside. In fact, research shows that many women find men without hair far more attractive than men with hair. Get yourself buffed up down the gym to remove any puppy fat from your cheeks, giving you a chiselled jawline to rival Batman. A goatee is also an option, but a full Michael Eavis beard that looks like your head's upside down is a step too far.

Some men who start to lose their hair early on can't imagine themselves without it. But within months of shaving your head people will be saying they can't imagine you with hair.

Some words of wisdom:

Accepting you're going bald is better for you in the long run than denying it to yourself for years. However, if it's really affecting your self-esteem talk to other family members who may have experienced the same thing.

How to survive your first Starbucks experience

When you first enter a Starbucks the bright lights and painfully jovial staff will be enough to make you feel nauseous, so the quicker you order the sooner you can get out of there.

Step 1 – Select your size. No matter what some people may say size does matter, in the world of coffee at least. The size simply means the number of caffeine or espresso shots – the stuff that makes you wide awake – each coffee has in it. There are three sizes:

Tall – one shot

Grande – (pronounced gran-day) two shots

Venti – (ven-tay) three shots

Step 2 – Choose your type of coffee.

☐ ESPRESSO – Slightly more than a thimble's worth of coffee. A pick-me-up for those on the go.

☐ LATTE – Pronounced lar-tay, this is the choice of the coffee novice. Roughly 80% hot milk, 20% espresso, the latte comes with a thin veil of tasteless milky foam on top.

☐ CAPPUCCINO – The cap-a-chi-no is exactly the same as a latte only with a mushroom cloud of foam topped with a sprinkling of cocoa powder and the promise of a milk moustache Magnum PI would be proud of.

☐ AMERICANO – Steaming hot water and espresso. Simple and effective. No surprise then that it's most men's weapon of choice for an early morning wake-up call.

☐ CAFÉ MOCHA – A latte hybrid with a spoonful of hot chocolate and whipped cream instead of the layer of foam. But sadly, no cocktail umbrella.

☐ CARAMEL MACCHIATO – For a man with a sweet tooth. Foamed milk, espresso, vanilla and caramel. Look out Tooth Fairy.

☐ FRAPPUCCINO – Milkshakes aren't just for kids, as this strong and frothy coffee escapade proves. Ice-blended versions of espresso, mocha, caramel macchiato and even a Starbucks special of strawberries and cream.

☐ VIVANNO – Feeling nutritional? Try a smoothie. Choose from orange, mango and banana or banana chocolate. Asking for an espresso to be added to the chocolate one is seen as respectable experimentation, ask for one to be added to the fruit one, however, and you're committing coffee blasphemy and could find your beans in the blender.

☐ TEA – From the spicy Tazo Chai that will tickle your nostril hair to the pot of Earl Grey straight from the pages of an Evelyn Waugh novel. If the complexities of coffee are getting you down, plump for a cuppa instead.

Step 3 – Practise your pronunciation and use of the terminology. Many of the baristas or servers may not be native English speakers, but they do speak the language of coffee. You need to be quick, as any inept mumbling or poor pronunciation can result in misunderstanding and humiliation.

Step 4 – Make the order. Keep it simple. Say the size followed by the type. For example: 'Tall latte, please.' The person behind the counter might try and catch you out at this point by saying, 'Would you like a pastry, sir?' Say 'No' in your kindest tone, grab your coffee and with 'Have a nice day!' ringing in your ears, get back among the grumps on the high street.

How to perform the perfect golf swing

Fig. 1. Overlapping

Yellow and red tartan bottom-hugging trousers, a gaudy sunvisor and a woolly tank top you wouldn't even wear as a dare on Christmas day ... On the golf course, however, it's not your jumper that will stick out like a sore thumb. Oh no. It's a bad swing. Perfect your swing and you can get away with any sartorial no-no.

Grip. Grasp the club with both palms facing one another. Place your left hand towards the top of the club grip, with your thumb pointing down, and place your right hand below but slightly over your left. Grip firmly but not too hard; hold the club in your fingers not your palms. Relax your wrists and keep your hands evenly matched on the club.

The three main grips:

Fig. 2. Baseball

* *Overlapping.* The little finger on the right hand sits in the groove of the index finger on the left hand. Good for those with strong forearms and wrists.

* *Interlocking.* The little finger on the right and the index finger on the left intertwine with each other. Suits those with fat and short hands.

* *Baseball.* All your fingers grip the handle like you're holding – funnily enough – a baseball bat. Fingers do not overlap or interlock but run alongside each other. For those with weak arms and strong wrists, or knitters.

Fig. 1.

Stance. Stand with your hips and feet positioned directly below your shoulders, with your feet pointing slightly out, not directly forward. Bend your knees as though you're perching on the edge of a table and lower your hips. Keep your back straight at all times. Your hands and arms should hang down from your shoulders with the club at the centre of your stance and your weight evenly spread.

Target alignment. When you are practising your swing, pick a target in the distance; something you can see out of the corner of your eye when you line up to the ball. A tall blade of grass, a tree, something immovable. You will need to concentrate on getting the target and aim correctly aligned, but with practice this will soon become second nature. Facing slightly to the left, align your body alongside the ball with the club and ball facing your target.

Fig. 2.

Backswing. Bend your elbows slightly towards you and slowly draw the club back over your shoulder. Shift your weight to your right foot. Simultaneously drop your left shoulder and lift your right. Don't consciously move your head, but allow the natural movement it makes to the right. Your right foot, hip and your head should be vertically inclined behind the ball. Your back should be facing the target and your shoulders at a right angle to your spine like a capital T. Keep your elbows close together. At the apex of the backswing your left arm should be stretched to the max across your chest and your right bent like a waiter's when carrying a tray on his shoulder. Your wrist should be hinged towards your neck with the club behind your head, pointing off in a straight line towards the ball.

Downswing. Allow your hips to run the show as they dip into the swing and pull your arms, which in turn will pull the club downwards. Don't move any other part of your body. Shift your weight from right to left early in the swing. Don't drag the club down; allow momentum to build until impact. The club should hit the ball at its maximum speed, thus optimizing the impact. Don't force it. Relax and be willing to let go and soon your swing will occur naturally.

Fig. 3.

Impact. An impact your right elbow should be pointing at your right foot and pretty much all your weight should be on your left foot. Rotate your hips through the motion. Your left arm will be straight by this point and your hands should be slightly in front of the ball. Your body will look like a K at impact, your left side straight and your right side bent in at the hip. Don't try to hit the ball hard – simply swing through it.

Follow through. Rotate your hips towards the target and let your upper body follow until all of you, apart from your feet and knees, face the target. Both arms stay straight at the beginning and then mimic the backswing in reverse, with the left arm bent more than the right. All your weight should be on your left foot. If you resemble a twisted Stretch Armstrong you know you've got it right.

Remember, practice makes perfect. Once you feel you're getting somewhere with your swing, congratulate yourself with a trip to the clubhouse shop and bag some tartan socks. It'll be the trousers next, and you know it.

When you first start to practise your swing, place a club on the ground, pointing the way you want the ball to go. Line your feet up with the shaft and strike the ball. This will help you avoid playing 'regimental golf' – hitting the ball left, right, left, right, left, right – rather than hitting it right up the middle of the fairway, where it's supposed to go.

Blagger's guide to apprentice slang

Whether your trade is plumbing, labouring, mechanics or retail, being the brunt of the jokes while you're an apprentice is part of the rites of passage on the path to becoming a major player in the company's future. The most common of all these practical jokes is getting sent to the local hardware shop to fetch a glass hammer or some rubber nails.

But if your mentor's being a little savvy you may well be sent out for one of the following:

* *Sky-hooks.* Being told to get hooks that hang in mid-air would normally be greeted with a smartass comment like, 'Who do you think I am? Paul Daniels?' but being eager to please can play tricks on the mind.

* *Skirting-board ladder.* Made out of matchsticks and cat hairs by the Borrowers, these pointless and completely non-existent items have given decorators wide eyes and slack jaws for years.

* *Stripy paint.* Apprentices will often return from going out for this red herring carrying two tins of emulsion. You'd think they'd cotton on once they crack the lids open.

* *A long weight.* This trickster's delight needs the complicity of a local shop. Upon arrival the apprentice is told to stand in the corner and wait. Too shy to ask, too nervous to leave, the long wait can be a very long one indeed.

How to behave in a job interview

You slave over your CV for days on end. Send it out to a hundred companies and after months of waiting, finally land that elusive interview. You buy a new suit. New pair of shoes. Get a haircut. And blow it all in an instant by swearing the minute you step through the door.

Here's how to make sure you raise a toast by getting the post:

Preparation:

* Research the company – products, services, market, trends, competitors – in B2B (business to business) magazines, on their website and in literature you can request prior to the interview.

* Prepare yourself for the generic questions. Why you want the job, what your strengths are, your best achievements, what you'd do if you got the job and a question to rival 'To be or not to be?' – 'Where do you see yourself in five years?'

* Find out the exact name of the person or persons who will be interviewing you. Arrive early and be polite to everyone in the building when you enter, especially the secretary. Her duties might go beyond the secretarial in nature. Wink, wink, nudge, nudge.

* Prepare a few questions for the company. Where they plan to be in the next few years shows an interest in their future. Also, take at least three spare copies of your CV in case you're asked to produce one.

* Dress smart. A suit and tie and shined shoes are a must no matter what the position. Casual dress gives the impression that you're a casual person.

*   If you smoke, don't smell of cigarettes on arrival and, it goes without saying, don't light up mid-question.

During the interview:

*   Walk in with a straight back, don't slouch, don't chew gum or look out of sorts; this is the moment you wished you'd passed on that final whisky chaser. Give a firm handshake on arrival to everyone in the room.

*   Body language. Face your interviewer. Don't cross your arms or legs and keep your head up and your hands still. Look the interviewer straight in the eye; thus making you look more confident and trustworthy.

*   Turn your mobile phone off. Never interrupt. Don't fidget. Don't look around the room and don't, no matter how itchy, scratch your groin.

*   Smile. Smiling is infectious and the chances are they'll take to you immediately. Either that or think you're a smug bastard who they'd never employ in a month of Sundays.

*   Don't use slang or go off on one. Control yourself and answer concisely and lucidly. Acknowledge the importance of the questions asked of you and relate each answer you give to the company in question.

*   Point out your strengths and don't be afraid to point out areas that you could progress in. If the position is a newly formed one, saying how you'd develop the role is paramount. Include innovation and invention in your ideas.

*   Be prepared for the dreaded 'What would you say are your weak points?' question. Be honest, but not too honest. And answering 'Well, sometimes I'm just too hard-working and a perfectionist' is just creepy.

Make your own cider

According to folklore, an apple is so much more than a juicy snack. One bite and Adam and Eve learned all about forbidden knowledge. One nibble and the Norse Gods earned the gift of immortality. Master the skill of cider making and you too can receive mystical powers in the comfort of your very own kitchen; the mystical powers of the piss artist.

You will need:

Apples. A selection of cider apples (Kingston Black, Foxwhelp, Golden Russet, etc) and dessert apples (Cox, Red Delicious, Worcester Pearmain, etc). Any apples will do but use a mix of eating and cider apples or the cider will be too sweet. Avoid cooking apples. 7.2kg or 16lb of apples will roughly make 3.75 litres or 1 gallon of cider.

Pulping device. A household blender or juicer, a Pulpmaster – a bucket with a rotating blade on the inside of the lid which attaches to a drill, they cost about £25 – or bucket and heavy object.

Cider press. You can purchase a professional job online but homemade efforts are just as good. Four large clamps, two hard flat surfaces, some muslin and a tray larger than the press are all you need.

A couple of sterilized buckets. Or kegs with lids and either a makeshift or real bunghole and bung. One bucket and one large plastic bottle will suffice.

Siphon. Or sterilized plastic tube.

Plastic or glass fermentation airlock.

Plastic or glass bottles. To hold the end product.

Optional:

Crown corker. For putting tops on the glass bottles.

Sachet of cider brewer's yeast.

Campden tablet. Used to aid the fermenting process.

Step 1. Wash apples in clear water. You can chop the apples in half at this point to see if any are rotten at the core. Discard bad apples.

Step 2. Pulp. Use your kitchen blender or juicer if you're making a couple of glasses for your grandma. Larger amounts require a Pulpmaster or if you don't have one, bludgeon your apples to a 'pomace' in a large bucket.

Step 3. Press. Place the large tray securely under the press. Wrap the pulp in the muslin cloth, place in the press and screw the clamps shut. The cloth stops the pulp from squelching all over the place and the large tray will catch all the juice. Loosening and tightening the screws will produce more juice.

Step 4. Fermenting. Fill your bucket or keg to the brim with the juice. At this point you have two choices:

* *Organic or Scrumpy Cider.* Leave the bunghole open. After 1–2 days wild yeast will naturally ferment the apples and white froth will bubble up through the hole. Organic can be hit and miss.

* *Brewer's Cider.* Add a Campden tablet. Two days later sprinkle a packet of yeast in. Place the airlock on top so no extra yeast gets in.

After two days the frothing and scum production will reduce but the fermentation carries on and ends roughly three weeks later.

Step 5. Racking off or *siphoning.* Place the bucket with the cider on an elevated surface and the other bucket or bottle below. Put one end of your siphon tube in the bunghole, suck on the other end and place in the lower bucket bunghole or bottle opening. This process siphons off the cider liquid leaving the dregs at the bottom of the cider called the 'lees'.

Step 6. Maturation. Remove the siphon tube. Place the airlock in the bunghole to keep flies etc. out but allow gas to escape. You can now leave your cider to mature for anything between three and eight months.

Step 7. Bottle up. Sterilize your bottles and siphon the cider into each one. If you want to seal each bottle use a crown corker to press the caps on. Store in a cool place.

How to complain in a restaurant *without looking like a complete prat*

Being British we'd probably rather die of food poisoning than complain. If you want to break from the national norm, follow these guidelines:

* Ensure what you're complaining about is valid. Getting angry because your starter is cold is a little sad if you ordered a chilled cucumber soup.

* Undercooked or missing ingredients are valid reasons to get mad and get even. Or just point the problem out politely.

* Voice your complaint ASAP. Eating half of your burger before demanding a new one will earn you a side order of 'homemade' mayonnaise when your plate is returned.

* Express what the problem is calmly and clearly. If it's not the waiter's problem, don't take it out on them. If it is, try to be nice. Bankers earn enough to be yelled at, waiters don't.

* Normally the waiter will take your food back to the kitchen and change it for you, however, if he is not forthcoming ask him if he could ask the chef to recook or redress your meal for you. Pressure him a little but smile and be polite.

* Sometimes service can be dreadful. If this is the case ask to see the manager and explain the problem factually. Don't just say the waiter looked at your girlfriend funny, especially if you are dining alone.

* If there's a problem with the bill, ask them to add it up again and check it meticulously.

How to fry the perfect steak

The steak is the Holy Grail of manhood, so take up the gauntlet and learn how to cook one like a trained chef. First of all, buy a fillet or sirloin steak from your local butcher's and take it home, preferably securing it with a seat belt or, better still, a baby seat.

Step 1. If your steak has been stored in the fridge, take it out half an hour or so before cooking and allow it to come to room temperature.

Step 2. Put either a chargrill or a heavy-based frying pan on the heat, get it really hot, but not smoking.

Step 3. Brush the steak with groundnut or olive oil or drizzle about a tablespoon of oil into the pan. Grind some salt and pepper over the steak to season.

Step 4. Place the steak in the pan. Fry the steak on one side, to seal it off, for about one to two minutes, depending on how you want it cooked, and then turn it over to cook the other side. Meanwhile warm your plate in the microwave for about 15 seconds.

Step 5. Once cooked, remove the steak from the pan and place on a rack or warm plate. Leave to rest for about five minutes in a warm spot before eating – this gives time for the meat to relax and your mouth to water. Plate up and tuck into a tender steak fit for King Arthur.

EXPERT TIP: A good way of testing if the steak is cooked to your liking is to use a simple finger test by comparing the springiness of the steak with the fleshy pad on your palm beneath the thumb, as shown. The softness of this part of your palm should match the texture of the meat following these simple thumb and finger combinations.

The Finger Test:

Little finger & thumb
Well done

Ring finger & thumb
Medium-to-well

Middle finger & thumb
Medium

Index finger & thumb
Rare

Open palm
Blue (i.e. completely raw)

Three fingers & thumb
Labrador steak

How to taste wine in a restaurant

If the waiter asks if you want to taste the wine you can either say you're happy for him to just pour it or, if you feel particularly confident, nod suavely.

* The waiter will pour you a quarter of a glass. Hold it up, tilt and check the colour. Both red and white wines should be translucent and jewel-like – never cloudy.

* Swirl the wine in the glass. **This adds oxygen to the wine – allowing it to 'breathe'** – and also lets you see the wine's 'legs' (Fig.1). These are the thin lines of liquid clinging to the side of the glass – which indicate the body and alcoholic strength of the wine. Lighter, less strong-bodied wines such as rosés will have a thinner consistency, and thus lighter 'legs'.

* Bring your glass to your nose and take a good sniff – **this is to test the aroma or 'nose' of the wine.** A slightly musty, or dusty smell, or a plainly unpleasant smell may indicate the wine is bad or 'corked'.

* Take a sip and let it get into the taste buds of your mouth. Swill it about your tongue and gums – but don't go all Jancis Robinson and start whittering about subtle blackberry and fire station overtones.

* Normally after tasting you'd spit the wine out, but not on this occasion. Just swallow and judge the 'finish' – the lingering taste of the wine. Unless you truly don't like how the wine tastes, ask for a glass to be poured.

This is a quick process so don't take an hour over it, you're going through the motions – they know you're not a wine connoisseur. Lift, swirl, smell, sip, swallow. As easy as ABC.

Fig.1. Nice legs

Striking the cue ball in pool:
how to generate different types of spin

The kid with the most kudos up at the local leisure centre was never the kid who could run the 100 metres in a nanosecond, or swim a whole length without coming up for air. It was the kid who could con the bar lady to give him a shot of rum in his coke, who could blow smoke rings and get the pool table to work with a well-positioned kick. Every leisure centre had one, and still does. Relive those halcyon pool days with some killer spin techniques the next time you're down the pub.

Topspin. This causes the cue ball to spin forward and run on after striking another ball. Strike the white ball a quarter of a cue tip directly above the centre. Keep the cue horizontal and avoid downward contact upon striking. Hitting the ball the slightest amount to the side of centre will also cause sidespin, so precision is the name of the game. **Hitting with more power won't make much difference. Follow through with the cue (Fig. 1).**

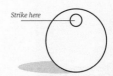

Fig. 1.

Backspin. Makes the cue ball spin back towards you after hitting a colour ball. Strike the ball at the base, below centre with some considerable force. Don't hit too low, about one and half cue tips is on the money. The greater the distance to the colour ball, the harder you should strike. After striking the ball, don't yank the cue back abruptly, instead, try to snap the cue forward sharply to get maximum impact. **Follow through and keep the cue parallel to the table (Fig. 2).**

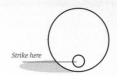

Fig. 2.

Sidespin. Generally used to change the direction of the cue ball when it hits the cushion. Sidespin also affects the direction a colour ball will take after impact with the cue ball. Hit the ball left of centre and the cue ball will move to the right slightly and vice versa. **The further out from centre you strike the ball the more the ball will curve (Fig. 3).**

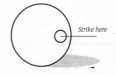

Fig. 3.

Stop shot. Does exactly what it says on the tin; when the ball collides with another ball it will stop in its tracks. Hit the ball slightly below centre – about a quarter of a cue tip. This should only take a small amount of draw, so don't whack it or you risk knocking some poor sod off their bar stool.

Jump shot. Get the right cue angle and you will make the ball do a little bunny hop, possibly over another ball. Elevate your cue and hit downwards on to the cue ball (Fig. 4).

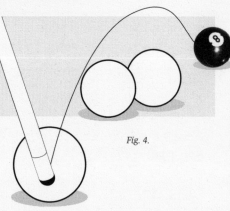

Fig. 4.

Masse shot. This shot will make the cue ball curve round the colour ball in front of it. Hold the cue almost vertically, directly above the ball. Strike the cue ball off centre. A fancy move but probably best left to Ronnie O'Sullivan and friends (Fig. 5).

Fig. 5.

Tip: you don't have to use these shots on their own. The real pro would be able to play a combination of top/back spin with sidespin. For example, by hitting the ball low – backspin – and to the right – sidespin – the white will come off the colour ball back, and to the right.

How to start a fire without matches or a light

Stranded on a desert island. Lost in the middle of a forest. Or merely messing about in the backyard after watching Ray Mears on the box. Men have an urge to master fire. And when there's no matches or lighters to hand you've got to do it the Neanderthal way.

Here's a selection of techniques to make sure your cockles don't get cold:

Hand drill

You will need:

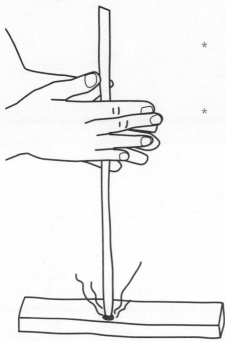

* Fireboard. A dry flat-ish piece of wood about a foot in length. Use a dry softwood such as willow, aspen or juniper.

* Spindle. A strong, thin and two-foot-long stick, preferably the same type of wood as the fireboard.

* Tinder nest. A bundle of super-dry small tinder such as grasses, seed heads, lichen, bark shavings from aspen, poplar, cottonwood trees. Form the bundle loosely to the size of a tennis ball.

The hand drill method relies on friction to create heat. Cut a V-shaped notch out of your fireboard. Place a piece of dry bark or sturdy leaf underneath the notch. With the spindle wedged into the notch rub your hands either side of the spindle, up and down applying a good amount of pressure. Keep going until a glowing ember falls onto the bark or leaf and transfer it to your tinder nest. Cup your hands around the nest and blow softly to fan the flame. Transfer the burning tinder to your prepared campfire.

Fire plough

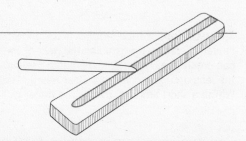

You will need:

* Fireboard

* Spindle

* Tinder nest

Another friction heat method. Cut a long groove down the centre of one end of the fireboard. Rub the spindle up and down the groove in firm, fast movements. Place your tinder nest at the end of the groove and once an ember forms it will fall into the nest and catch fire. Continue as above.

Bow drill

You will need:

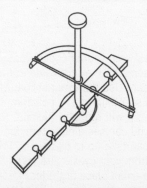

* Fireboard

* Spindle

* Tinder nest

* Socket. A heavy rock of some kind

* Bow. A bendy stick, at least as long as your arm

* String. In true survival fashion a shoelace will suffice

Create your bow by tying one end of the string to one side of the bow. Loop the string around your spindle and tie the loose end to the other side of the bow. Cut a notch in the fireboard. Place the spindle into the notch and apply pressure on top of the spindle with the socket. Saw back and forth with the bow. This rotates the spindle quickly and an ember should form as with the hand drill method.

Lens method

You will need:

* A pair of glasses, magnifying glass, piece of glass, etc.

* Sunlight

* Tinder nest

This technique will be familiar to anyone who cruelly burned ants to a cinder at school. By focusing the heat of the sun on one specific spot you can create fire. Place the lens under the sun and over your tinder nest. Tilt the lens until you can see a clear beam – a clear silver dot – on the tinder. Within a short amount of time the tinder will spark.

Can and chocolate method

You will need:

* Coke or other drink can

* Chocolate bar with foil wrapper

* Sunlight

* Tinder nest

* Tweezers

Unwrap your chocolate bar and smear some on the underside of the Coke can. Use the wrapper to buff the metal. Essentially you're polishing the surface so it will rebound the sun. Repeat until you can see a clear reflection of your face in the can – have patience this can take up to two hours. Point the bottom of the can at the sun – away from your eyes – and using a pair of tweezers (to reduce the shadows) hold a small piece of tinder directly in the reflected beam, about 2cm from the centre of your can bottom. Once the piece of tinder begins to smoke, transport to your tinder nest.

Tip: Toothpaste, or ashes, will work just as well to polish the can. Rub it in with a cloth.

Battery and steel wool method

You will need:

* 9 volt battery

* Steel wool

* Tinder nest

Stretch the steel wool out. Rub the side of the battery with the nub, or contacts, on the steel wool. The wool will glow as it gets hotter. Blow softly to keep the wool glowing – it will cool quickly – and place in your tinder nest.

Tinder fungus: In the UK, the most common form of tinder fungus is also known as King Alfred's Cake fungus. This corky growth is found on birch barks, and is one of the few naturally found materials that will catch a spark and glow readily.

Get hold of a chunk of tinder fungus and keep small dry bits in a small tin. Keep this in your pocket at all times, just in case you need to start a fire.

A whole large fungus will also retain a glow over a long period, so that it can be transported and used to make a fire in a new camp. Cut a large fungus in half, and use one half as a lid to keep the glow alight.

How to sharpen a knife using a whetstone

Whether you're in training for Masterchef or just peeling a few spuds for tea, every chef needs a good sharp knife. Sharpening knives is all about angles – yet another reason why you should have paid more attention in maths class.

Here's how to do it like Marco Pierre White:

1. Your whetstone has a rough side and a smooth side. Rub the rough side with mineral oil or water to remove small particles that could clog up the stone and ruin the grind. (Water on a water stone, oil on an oil stone. Don't mix and match the two.)

2. Place your thumb tightly on top of the handle of the knife and push the blade – lengthways – in a short and steady motion away from you at the preferred angle. Between 22 and 25 degrees – the angle your knife would be at if you were to rest it against a box of matches – is the standard angle for sharpening European knives. For Japanese and professional fillet knives, hold the knife at an angle between 12 and 15 degrees. This scrapes away the metal to form a blunt edge, or burr, the first step to sharpening your knife. Never pull the knife towards you or you risk losing a finger or two.

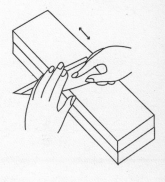

3. Feel for the burr every now and then. Put your thumb on the other side of the edge you've been grinding and gently slide downwards along the flat side. You should feel something scraping at your skin – this is the burr. The burr will form quicker nearer the hilt but take longer towards the tip. Keep grinding until the burr is formed all along the blade.

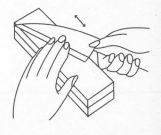

4. Once you establish a burr on one side grind away on the other so that the burr covers the entire length. You need to get a burr on either side.

5. Turn the stone over so the fine side is facing up. Slightly raise the angle of the knife and continue to grind away as before; this will remove the burr and leave you with an über-sharp micro bevel – the edge of the blade.

6. Take it slow and alternate sides moving from the hilt all the way down to the tip. Release the pressure as you go and once you've done ten strokes on either side check the sharpness by holding a piece of newspaper and seeing if it goes through it with ease.

7. Keep going until the blade is sharpened equally.

8. Finally, with no pressure at all, lift the angle ever so slightly and glide down the stone to finish.

9. Wipe the stone clean at the end of each sharpening session.

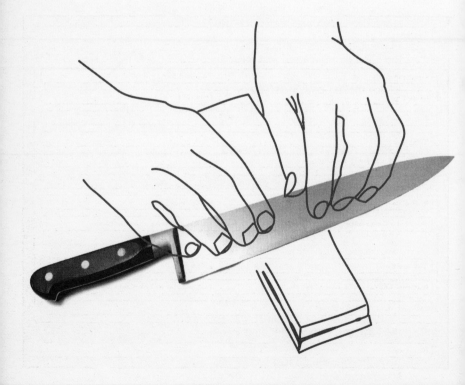

Understanding your payslip

*For most men, the arrival of their payslip means one thing –
time to hit the pub. But before you drink your way back into
overdraft, why not open the envelope and at least attempt to
understand what all those codes and jargon mean?*

**Every payslip layout differs from workplace to workplace.
However, the essentials are as follows:**

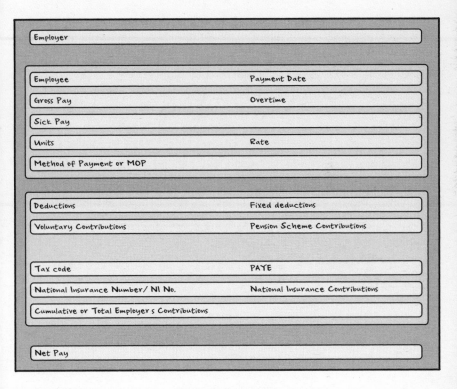

Employer. Name of the company you work for.

Employee. Your name ... unless you've mistakenly got your boss's pay
slip. Should also have your employee number, to quote to your accounts
department if you have any queries re. your payslip.

Payment Date. When you'll receive the money.

Gross Pay. Your full pay without any additional hours or deductions.

Overtime. Any extra hours you've put in out of sheer love for your chosen vocation.

Sick Pay. Days you've taken off sick because England is playing in the World Cup.

Units. Hours of work you've done.

Rate. How much you earn per hour. Or the depressing bit.

Method of Payment or MOP.

* BACS, or Banker's Automated Clearing Services. The money is paid directly into your bank or building society account.

* Cash. Cold hard wonga.

Deductions. A list of deductions from your gross pay.

Fixed deductions. Always the same. States the amount, what it is for and how often deducted.

Voluntary Contributions. Savings scheme, charity donation, staff gym membership, sack the boss campaign etc.

Pension Scheme Contributions. A percentage of your income you put aside for your future pension.

* LGPS – Local Government Pension Scheme.

* Pension contribution – pension contributions from your salary for the current year.

* AVC – Additional Voluntary Contributions to a pension scheme.

PAYE. Stands for Pay As You Earn income tax. Your employer pays a percentage of your income as income tax directly to the Inland Revenue, unless you are self-employed or freelance.

Tax code. The letter in the code will be L unless you have two jobs when the code will be D0. The amount depends on what income and if you earn less than £36,000 you pay 20%, or BR, basic rate tax.

National Insurance Number/NI No. Your unique identification number, automatically allocated to everyone born and living in the UK. For use in all dealings with Inland Revenue and Customs, the Social Security Agency in NI or the Department for Work and Pensions. If you have recently arrived in the UK and do not have a NI number, you must be over 16 to apply for one if making claims or if you are employed.

National Insurance Contributions. A compulsory contribution to fund the welfare state, which encompasses state pensions and the NHS. But sadly not Sky Sports.

Cumulative or Total Employer's Contributions. A total of the National Insurance and Income Tax payments made from the start of the tax year, April, to the current date.

Net Pay. Your take home pay, minus deductions. The total amount you'll receive in a pay packet, or paid directly into your bank account.

Acknowledgements

All the blokes in my life – and a few blokettes – who've filled out questionnaires, lent their words of wisdom and put up with my ego trips. They include: Dan Ward, Lenny Teehan, Joey Card, Dave McAllister, Luke Elms, Tony Ambler, Trist Earl, Andy Palmer, Katie Hall, Lambert Kleinjans, Amy Mann, Niki Khouroushi, Mikey 'Man's Man' Holroyd and everyone at Drake Circus Waterstone's, especially Clint 'I hate Bret Hart' Jones.

For various gems of information from the sublime to the serious I'd like to thank Olly Luscombe, Neil Parker, Phil Jane, Jayne Morris, the guys at Slow Dating, the Japanese waitress in Yukisan, numerous Starbucks employees, all at David May Motor Services, South Devon Women's Aid, the two very friendly women in Blackheath, and Daisy at the Spearmint Rhino in Sheffield. Also, all my ex girlfriends – without whom this book wouldn't have had half the insight it does. Sorry for all the grief and thank you for all the patience.

To all those who supported me with my idea for 'a manual for young men' from beginning to end a massive thanks goes to all the staff on the Professional Writing course at University College Falmouth. Including Tom Scott, Susy Marriot and Christina Bunce – this book wouldn't exist if it weren't for you three. For help with the website and various other bits and bobs: Matt Collins, Tony Bowry, Paul Matchett, Cam, Laura Sewell, Dena Blakeman, Merik Flynn, Luke Friend, Katy Moon, Kate Burt, Fiona 'Iolaire' Campbell-Howes, James 'DM' Henry and everyone else I've undoubtedly missed out. An extra big thank you to Pat and Rog – we'll always have Whitstable.

At Random House I'd like to thank my editor Rosemary Davidson whose insight and vision has taken this book beyond anything I could have imagined. Thanks for putting your faith in a young author. For Tom in editorial, Tom in sales, Louise Rhind-Tutt in publicity, Claire Morrison in marketing and all the phantom proofreaders and supporters. Thank you to all the designers and illustrators at Unreal who nailed the sentiment of the book from the word go and brought all the tips to life in a way just words couldn't have.

My agent Susan Smith deserves a singular thank you. Thanks for putting up with my rants and raves whether work related or relationship related. You're not only a great agent but also a great friend. Just promise me you'll stay away from kayaks and Burgh Island!

A little thanks to my two A-level English Lit teachers, Ms Daniel and Mr Dart. Never be a writer eh?

And last but not least my family. Uncle Col for his beard and horse racing advice, Auntie Biddy for her permanent interest and unfaltering support. Rex, Ad, Suzy, Catharine, Glynn, Cal, P, M and B for always showing an interest. My sister and her three little boys – Ben, Wills and Edward – for teaching me how to hold a baby, not to mention all her invaluable advice at pivotal moments in my life over the past year. Her husband and my brother-in-law Mick for everything car, Beckham and beer related. For my late Grandma and Nanny who taught me the importance of compassion with their tales of sandbags, American soldiers and air-raid shelter shenanigans. To my parents, who have supported me in every way, shape and form in achieving this and always encouraged me to follow my dream when most would have told me it was time to call it a day. 'Golden Balls' would like to thank you and ensure you both you've passed the nursing home test with flying colours!

Gareth May

Penryn, Cornwall; August 2009

About the author

Born and bred in Devon, Gareth is a twenty-something writer. In 2007, he set up the popular blog 21st-Century-Boy.co.uk, with the intention of giving young men an alternative voice from the lad-mag generation, and his humorous but informative videos have had 100,000s of views on YouTube. Gareth likes listening to the cricket on the wireless, drinking ale and watching *Midsomer Murders*. And is well aware that all three make him an incredibly old git.